VERY GOOD Car Stories

Lots of things to read about cars… and the people who drive them

By Simon Heptinstall

Other books to avoid,
also by Simon Heptinstall:

The Big Book of Car Trivia

Car Miscellany

Car Marques

1001 Dream Cars

What on earth is in this book anyway?

Well...
Do you know who is the world's fastest blind driver and what is the Taliban's own supercar like?
Or who spent 50 years driving an electric egg and why was a German teenage driver banned 49 minutes after passing his test?

The VERY GOOD Car Stories book has quite a few stories almost as good as these.
Top Gear writer Simon Heptinstall's last book of car trivia was widely praised (by his family). This one is nearly as good.

VERY GOOD Car Stories
By Simon Heptinstall

Published by: Very Good Books
Cover photo: ©Arkonik/James Cheadle
(It's a lovely Arkonik Land Rover Defender photographed at the waterfront in Bristol. Thanks to Arkonik for letting me use it.)

ISBN: 9798865342496

The VERY GOOD Car Stories book starts here

This book is dedicated to my grey 2008 Volvo C30 2.0 petrol.

My Swedish coupe/hatchback uses an engine designed by Mazda, and in my car, it is paired with a Ford gearbox.

This Mazda engine fitted to my car is also used in the Mazda MX-5 and Mazda 6, Ford Focus, Mondeo and Transit, various Volvos, Chinese Bestune B70 saloons, Zenos mid-engined sportscar, seven different types of Caterham, Morgan Plus4, the rare Mitsuoka Roadster, GInetta G40 and the Taatuus F4-T014 junior formula single-seat racing car.

The Volvo is unique however in its special patented body structure ingeniously designed to absorb impacts – by using body panels composed of a mix of four different types of steel.

Volvo means 'I roll' in Latin.

Contents

VERY GOOD Car Stories

This is a VERY BIG book so of course you may need to keep referring to this contents page or you may get hopelessly lost.

First gear
From vision-free motoring…
to a swastika paint-job

1 Who is the world's fastest blind driver?

I have to start the book somewhere and this is as good a place as any because it sums up what I find interesting about motoring – it's the story of the world's champion blind driver. Former bank manager Mike Newman of Bolton, England, was born blind… but now has the unlikely title of the planet's fastest blind driver.

While still working at a bank he set the word record for blind driving – by taking a Jaguar XJR to 144mph (232kph) in 2003 at off-road testing track.

He has since beaten his own record three times. His latest speed run achieved 200mph (322kph) in a Nissan GTR. Mike drives on the empty airfield alone but had a live radio link to a 'navigator' in a car following him – to warn if he was veering off course.

He now runs track days for disabled drivers using two dual-control buggies – which he has named after his two guide dogs for the blind. "I've always been car-mad," says Mike.

2 Soup defender

One of the weirdest road stories of the last few years was the report of the driver from New Orleans, USA, who was pictured in 2023 on CCTV – bravely fighting off a carjacker by flinging a pot of hot soup at him.

The smartly dressed motorist was shown parking after buying a take-away local gumbo soup. He looks back over his shoulder to see a stranger getting into his smart red SUV.

The driver, in a light grey suit, races back to his car and throws his soup through the open sunroof at the carjacker inside.

The thief manages to escape through the vehicle's far door, covered in soup – and our hero recovers his car, albeit with some soup stains to clean up.

3 You crazy diamond

A struggling F1 team, a rookie driver and US$250,000-worth of diamonds mounted on a racing car's bonnet... what could possibly go wrong?

It was in the 2004 Monaco Grand Prix that Jaguar Racing got somehow embroiled in a promotion for the new Hollywood movie Ocean's Twelve. For some bizarre reason this involved placing fabulous diamonds on the car's nosecone.

Surprise, surprise – the car, with rookie Christian Klien at the wheel – crashed on the very first lap. The Jag smashed straight into a wall and Klein was unhurt.

The car was later recovered by crane – and guess what? Nobody knows where those button-sized diamonds went. They vanished from the scene... and are still missing.

4 Your Tube

A 1911 Rolls Royce Silver Ghost Limousine included a separate compartment for the chauffeur who could communicate with his passengers via a special speaking tube.

5 Bare offence

German motorists are legally allowed to be completely naked while driving. The car is considered a 'private space' in German law. Emerging from a vehicle naked is illegal however, so nude drivers have to quickly put something on when re-entering a 'public space'.

6 The official dummy

Official crash testing dummies represent an adult male who is 5ft 9ins tall and weighs 171lbs/12 stone 3lbs.

7 Parking incentive

A car-park owner in Cornwall, England, has introduced a unique two-tier pricing system – based on the ability of the driver to park properly.

Official signs at the entrance from the road announce that the Portheras Cove car park charges a standard £3 for 'parking neat and tight'. The price rises to £10 however – for 'parking like a wally'.

8 Wizard loses its power

In 1931 the new Hillman Wizard was launched in Britain as a direct challenge to "the American type of car."

The Rootes brothers' first six-cylinder Hillman featured the latest transatlantic styling, with chrome-plated front and rear bumpers and a curvy pressed steel body. It was "the car for the roads of the world" claimed the advertising.

However a newspaper road test found that the 2.8-litre saloon could only reach a paltry 65 mph (105kph) when it was flat out. The Wizard consequently did not sell as well as hoped. Production was soon curtailed and it was quickly replaced in the Rootes line-up.

9 Ooops, wrong car

Virginia police vehicles surrounded and then violently rammed a private car head-on – before realising it was the wrong car. In fact the vehicle contained an innocent young mother doing her shopping with a one and five-year-old child. The mystified mother was handcuffed at gun-point before police started realising they could've made a huge mistake and began profusely apologising, according reports of the 2022 incident.

10 Hidden treasures

An unlikely museum has opened in the strict Islamic state of Iran – and it contains some of the world's oddest cars.

The Iran Historical Cars Museum in the outskirts of Tehran exhibits the 55 vehicles owned by the fabulously wealthy Iranian Royal family before it was ousted by the 1979 Islamic Revolution.

After 50 years of being kept in secret storage the collection is now drawing thousands of locals to see what lavish lives the Shah and his retinue once enjoyed.

The cars include a one-off Mercedes gifted by Adolf Hitler and an American 1930's limousine with a gold-plated bumper and headlights. At the time, this Pierce-Arrow Model A with gold crests on the doors cost around an eighth of the entire national budget of Iran.

Perhaps the highlight of the collection is a one-off 1972 bright orange 'MPV Tehran'. It was an odd buggy-type single-seater produced jointly by VW, Porsche and Mercedes.

The car was a gift to the Shah – just to allow his 12-year-old son, the Crown Prince, to learn to drive. It came with two keys. A solid silver one limits the output to 18mph (30kph) – while using a gold key allows adults to drive and the engine to reach a more grown-up 105mph (170kph).

11 Driverless taxi

China's first robot taxi service opened in 2022. Baidu Apollo self-driving cars now give lifts to paying passengers around the 3.5 square miles/9 square kilometres of Beijing's Shougang Park – with the added bonus of no cab driver asking for a tip at the end.

12 Beatle Gets Back

Sir Paul McCartney recently took part in a filmed recreation of the famous scene where he and the Beatles walked across a zebra crossing outside Abbey Road Studios in London, England. The image formed the cover of the group's 1969 album 'Abbey Road'.

However when McCartney, now aged 80, was being filmed on the crossing, a stranger's car sped down the street, refused to stop at the crossing and almost flattened the ageing pop star. His daughter Mary told reporters she saw the humorous side to it: "It was so funny because the car nearly ran him over."

13 Escaping global disaster

When a police deputy in Florida, USA, caught a car that raced right through a stop sign at 20mph above the speed limit he found that the driver had an unique excuse. He was fleeing imminent nuclear war.

The excuse was caught on the officer's webcam and widely spread on social media. The unnamed driver is heard saying: "The truth is I just found out that Putin says he's going to launch thermonuclear war against the world. I was just trying to get back to my house to find out what is going on. I'm freaking out here. I got people in Ukraine."

14 Bond cars

Car enthusiast Alan Bond of Worthing, UK, has a unique collection of Bond three-wheeler minicars from the seventies. The distinctive 700cc two-seater normally came in bright orange and was nicknamed the Bond Bug.

Alan normally drives a Land Rover but bought the two Bonds because they matched his surname. "They're actually bloody awful to drive," he says.

15 Stick to the limit

In 1905 Rolls Royce built a luxury 3.5-litre V8 car with a top speed limited to just 20mph (32kph) – because that's what the UK speed limit was at the time.

16 Declining cars

Almost one in seven (14%) UK drivers are considering getting rid of their car, rising to one in three (35%) under 34s.

According to a new survey of UK drivers, over half (56%) say they do not need a car as much as they once did. Drivers were also thinking about down-sizing their vehicles, with over a quarter (26%) saying their next car is probably going to be smaller.

17 Battery supercars

An electric-powered supercar can be just about as powerful as you want as long as the battery is big enough.

So nobody doubts the performance claims of a new EV hypercar from an Italian company called Mobili Estrema – and journalists are unlikely to ever get a chance to test them out. The exotic two-door Fulminea offers an outrageous 2,040hp, all-wheel-drive and astonishing acceleration of 0-200mph (320kph) in under ten seconds.

The Fulminea is evidently limited to 217mph/350kph and the range is an impressive 323 miles/520km.

The car was launched in summer 2023 with a limited production run of 61 vehicles destined for mega-rich owners as each costs a cool £2m/$2.5m.

18 Top tyre team

The biggest tyre manufacturer in the world is not Michelin, Pirelli or Dunlop. It's Lego.

19 Ten car 'jokes'

Website boredpanda.com gathered 114 jokes about cars.
A few were funny.

Here are some of the best:

• The worst thing about parallel parking is witnesses.
• My lifetime boycott of Ferrari and Lamborghini is still going strong… And will continue until they lower the price.
• What kind of cars do people in Norway drive? Fjords.
• I just got nine out of 10 on my driver's test. The last guy was able to get out of the way.
• The biggest irony is being hit by a Dodge.
• What's the best part of Audi's customer service? They answer within four rings.
• What do you call a guy who always loses his car? Carlos.
• What do you get when dinosaurs crash their cars? Tyrannosaurus wrecks.
• I couldn't work out how to fasten my seatbelt. Then it clicked.
• Wanted: A man who has been stealing wheels from police cars. Police are working tirelessly to catch him.
• As I put my car in reverse, I thought to myself... "Ah, this takes me back."

20 Post-war bubble

The German car industry was decimated by the Second World War. Afterwards metal was very rare and fuel strictly rationed. Resurgent car manufacturers adapted to create a new breed of vehicle – the microcar.

These ultra cheap, light, tiny and economical vehicles were known affectionately as 'bubble cars'.

Bubble cars are now sought-after by collectors. The most desirable is the four-wheeled FMR (Messerschmitt) TG500 Tiger. This was the sportiest bubble car, with a 500cc two-stroke twin-cylinder engine twice as big as its rivals. It could accelerate, slowly, to 80mph/129 kph.

Only 320 TG500s were produced and less than half still exist. They are the most prized bubble cars and rarely appear at auction.

The record price was one of these Tiger microcars was for a rose-coloured 1958 model that fetched more than the price of a Lamborghini Huracan - a massive £255,000/$322,000 in 2013. This is the most expensive two-stroke vehicle ever sold.

* Only four motorbikes with two-stroke engines are in the top 250 most valuable motorcycles ever sold at auction. Three of them were owned by Steve McQueen (two Husqvarna dirt bikes and a Scott Flying Squirrel, which was the highest seller at £218,000/$276,000) and the other is a world-title-winning Aprilia RSW250.

21 The Bentley Babe

Well-built, with dashing features and slicked-back dark hair, Woolf 'Babe' Barnato was a perfect example of the flamboyant thirties playboy motor racer.

He inherited a fabulous fortune, dated heiresses – and was actually an amazing racing driver too. In fact his 100% record of three wins in three entries in the Le Mans 24 Hour Race stands as an unbeatable tribute.

He was born in the royal enclave of St James, London, and when his father died two years later (officially 'death by drowning while temporarily insane') he inherited a vast South African diamond and gold mining fortune.

After Charterhouse public school and Trinity College Cambridge, Barnato became a prize-winning motorboat racer, heavyweight boxer and played golf with a close friend of King Edward VIII. He was a Royal Artillery Captain in the First World War, then played county cricket as wicketkeeper for Surrey.

In the twenties he suddenly took an interest in motorsport. He bought a new Bentley, then a year later bought the company. Barnato became one of the notorious 'Bentley Boys', an unofficial group of rich ex-military playboys who drove, drank and lived fast. Their Bentleys would appear outside parties in swanky London addresses, blocking the road and causing traffic chaos.

Barnato's devil-may-care attitude seemed to make him a fearless driver though. He won many races at Brooklands and set a new 24-hour world speed record. W.O. Bentley described him as "the best driver we ever had."

To prove it, in 1928, 1929 and 1930 Barnato entered the Le Mans 24-Hour race – and won it each time in a different Bentley. No driver has ever matched that feat.

The classic Barnato story is of the time he sat in the bar at the Carlton Hotel, Cannes on the French Riviera in March 1930. He bet someone £100 that driving his 6.5-litre Bentley he could out-race the famous French Le Train Bleu express train – not only from Cannes to Calais but he could be across the Channel and back in his club in London before the train even got to Calais.

He set off at 6pm, a little after the train left (he said he was finishing his drinks first) and arrived in Boulogne at 10.30am the next morning despite a puncture and heavy rain. He had to wait for the 11.30 ferry but still parked in front of The Conservative Club in St James by 3.20pm, four minutes before the Blue Train reached Calais.

Barnato won the bet but French authorities fined him far more than the winnings for 'racing on public roads'.

His life continued in much the same vein, marrying three times (twice to wealthy American heiresses), becoming a RAF Wing Commander in the Second World War and having a spectacular Thames-side house built in Surrey in 1938 that featured a heated pool, a cinema for 'talkie' films and ahead-of-its-time central heating. He also owned an island in Bermuda.

At his funeral in 1948 the cortege was led by his classic racing Bentley, known as 'Old Number One', covered in flowers. The Sports Car Club of America was so moved it named its highest annual accolade the Woolf Barnato Award in his honour. It is still presented to a major figure in motorsport every year.

22 Car chase flop

In 2022 a man who stole a Mazda 6 saloon in the centre of the Spanish capital Madrid tried to mimic dramatic chase scenes from movies – escaping pursuers by driving through huge double doors into the city bus station and driving down a wide staircase.

The grim reality however involved him getting the car completely stuck between the handrails of the stairs. The thief then tried another movie classic: escaping through the car side window – but in reality it took so long to squeeze through he was easily caught by police. The white Mazda eventually had to be winched back up the staircase by firemen.

23 Royal motors

King Charles III is the biggest car enthusiast in the British Royal family.

One of his proudest possessions is a blue Aston Martin DB6 Volante given to him by his mother, the then Queen Elizabeth, more than 50 years ago on his 21st birthday. In 2008 he felt that the Aston could do with an eco-make-over so he had the engine modified to run on by-products from the British wine and cheese industries.

In 2019, Charles also purchased one of the first all-electric Jaguar I-Pace cars seen in the UK. He sometimes uses the I-Pace for official duties to minimise air pollution – although sometimes he uses a horse and carriage and sometimes a helicopter too.

Charles also inherited his mother's state limousine, a Bentley that she received from the manufacturer in celebration of her 50th anniversary on the throne in 2002. When the reigning monarch is abroad, the Bentley ornament on the bonnet is replaced with a silver sculpture of St George slaying the dragon.

* Whenever she had the chance, the late Queen was more than happy to jump behind the wheel herself.

One of Elizabeth's favourite vehicles was a Vauxhall Cresta PA Friary Estate, which was tailored to her outdoors needs and hobbies. It included features like a dog guard for her corgis, a gun rack for pheasant shooting and fishing-rod holders on the car's roof.

24 Bizarre brakes

A car's parking brake, called a handbrake in the UK, was usually operated by a level between the two front seats.
In some Porsche 911s it operated awkwardly via a lever between the driver's seat and the door – or by a knob on the dashboard in a VW Transporter.
Many American cars operate the parking brake by using an extra pedal mounted in the driver's footwell. More recently an electronic button-operated parking brake has become a common fitment.
* Some rally cars have a special hydraulic brake for the rear wheels that is operated by a level that is so long it almost reaches the steering wheel. It allows driver's to do quick handbrake turns to throw the back of the car round a corner.

25 Car-theft vigilante

There were huge community protests in Washington DC, USA, after a homeowner shot dead an unarmed 13-year-old boy he thought was breaking into his car early in 2023.

26 What does it mean when a car is a two-litre?

The measure of the 'engine's displacement' is a volume measurement that often is used to describe the type or model of car.

It is a measurement of the volume inside the engine cylinders that is swept by the pistons. This means it is working part of all the combined cylinders, where combustion of fuel and air takes place. It doesn't include the combustion chamber where the spark ignites the fuel or the pistons themselves or any of the valves.

It's a shorthand way of describing roughly the size, thirst and power of an engine, although these can vary through lots of other factors like turbocharging or compression ratio.

This displacement measurement is usually stated in metric units, either cubic centimetres for a 500cc engine or litres for a 3.5-litre engine for example.

Confusingly, in the US many use imperial measurements to describe engine size. This means an engine is often described in cubic inches of displacement. This means a two-litre engine would be called a 122 cubic inch motor in America.

The world of motor journalism is haunted by the complicated sum to convert from cubic inches to cubic centimeters. It involves multiplying by 16.39.

27 Dumped cars

Recent research across all British local authorities found that there are an astonishing 21,106 cars reported as being left abandoned every year in the UK.

The commonest abandoned vehicles are Ford Transit, Vauxhall Astra and Ford Focus. The towns with the most abandoned vehicles are Bradford, Milton Keynes and Barnet.

28 Wrong lane peril

Drivers who accidentally use the wrong lane on a stretch of American highway may be fined thousands of dollars.

Multi-lane road systems cross the border between Mexico and USA at spots like Tijuana. They could provide the opportunity for the most costly wrong-lane decisions in the world.

Sat nav systems direct drivers via the fastest lane but those who don't pay careful attention may get into a special fast-track lane for pre-booked vehicles. Drivers incorrectly using this lane are fined up to $10,000 by eagle-eyed border officials.

29 Biggest motor

At the time of writing, the largest car engine available on any production car is an 8.4-litre Viper V10 engine produced by Chrysler. The standard untuned V10 produces a massive 640 horsepower, which when fitted to a Viper can take it from 0-60mph in 2.96 seconds, before hitting a top speed of 205mph/330kph.

30 Taliban Toyota

The Taliban of Afghanistan has unveiled its own supercar. The Mada 9 was revealed at a ceremony in Kabul to astonished journalists who have often characterised the Taliban as a semi-terrorist organisation in the past.

The low-slung two-door Mada prototype coupe, powered by a highly-tuned Toyota Corolla engine, will help boost the Afghan regime's international image said officials.

31 Star's Volvo estate

Actor Paul Newman owned a boxy old grey 1988 Volvo 740 estate car that he transformed into a unique performance machine for everyday driving by fitting it with a turbocharged Buick V6 engine and the gearbox from a Pontiac Firebird.

* Rock star Chris Rea, also a motorsport fanatic, drives a hot-tuned Volvo estate too.

32 Irish car-maker

The Shamrock was a little-known car produced in County Monaghan, Ireland in the late 1950s. It was an idea financed by American businessmen who thought an Irish car would sell well among America's Irish immigrant population.
Sadly the big American-style convertible car used a tiny 1.5-litre Austin engine with weedy performance and only ten were built before the factory closed. Locals say all the unused parts were promptly dumped in the local lake.

33 Charge fine

Australian EV owners can be fined up to $3,200 (US$2,130/£1745) if they are caught blocking a public charger if they aren't currently using it.

34 Car cat caution

A survey in America in 2023 found the cars most likely to have their catalytic convertors stolen:
10 Chevrolet Cruze
9 Toyota Tacoma
8 Chevrolet Silverado
7 Chevrolet Equinox
6 Ford Econline
5 Ford Explorer
4 Honda CRV
3 Toyota Prius
2 Honda Accord
1 Ford F-Series Pickup

35 Super-watch

A premium watch produced by Aston Martin went on sale in 2023 costing more than a standard family hatchback car. The Girard-Perregaux Laureato Green Ceramic Aston Martin Edition costs US$25,800/£21,146.

36 Heater switch

The Pagani Zonda supercar uses a climate control unit that was originally fitted to the humble Rover 45.

37 Fake tickets

A Californian teenager printed out fake parking tickets as part of an ingenious scam to defraud motorists. The 19 year-old was caught red-handed by police putting his homemade tickets on cars around Santa Cruz beaches in 2023. The realistic tickets feature a QR code that lead to a home-made website to pay the fine.

The website was of course set up by the teenage boy to accumulate the fines for himself but none were paid and instead he was arrested and charged.

38 Most powerful motor

Although the Chrysler V10 that I wrote about a few pages ago is physically bigger with a larger displacement, the most powerful production car engine in the world currently is Bugatti's 8.0-litre W16.

And not only is it the most powerful production engine ever – it's also the most complex, boasting 64 valves and four turbochargers.

Its W-shaped 16-cylinder layout has been described as "essentially an orgy between two massive V8s". The W has an output of more than 1,000bhp and a somewhat enormous 1,250Nm of torque.

39 Cycle twist

Vancouver cyclist Ben Bollinger was hit by a driver than ignored a stop sign – but ending up being charged $3,700 to repair the car that hit him.

The Canadian cyclist was hit while pedalling on a cycle path when he was hit by an apparently out-of-control car. It sent him flying about 50 feet. His injuries included a broken hand and foot.

However, a complex new British Columbia motoring law includes the stipulation that all residents can claim benefits for damages after a crash, regardless of who was to blame. This creates a loophole that means that as Bollinger was uninsured but the driver of the car was insured, the cyclist has to pay for all the damages caused.

40 In-car entertainment

Daimler and Marconi conducted the first known experiments with car radios in 1922.

They involved fitting bulky receiving equipment with glass valves inside two cars, which also had frame-mounted aerials fitted to roof.

The cars then drove between the Strand in London and the broadcasting station in Essex. Occupants listened on individual 'ear telephones'.

The Times correspondent reported that "gramophone records were heard with ease and the speed of the car seemed to make no difference."

He said that "the interesting development foreshadows the possibility that the occupants of motor-cars may be able to listen to wireless concerts while travelling along the roads."

41 Bugatti block

Bugatti has designed a luxury apartment block in Dubai. The 46-storey building will include a special lift system to bring residents' cars up to viewing rooms next to their apartments.

42 Rudest car owners

A UK poll ranked the rudest and most polite drivers by the brand of car they drive. The result was very conclusive. Half of the entire vote chose BMW drivers as the rudest.

In detail, BMW owners were voted the most likely to hog the middle lane (according to 38 per cent of respondents), brake suddenly to scare the person behind (34 per cent), overtake (25 per cent) and not merge until the very last minute (35 per cent).

They are also considered to be the drivers most likely to honk at someone for going too slowly (37 per cent), pip the horn as soon as the traffic lights change to green (36 per cent), give the middle finger (38 per cent) and not pull over for emergency vehicles (31 per cent).

The full poll results:

Rudest drivers
1 BMW 50%
2 Audi 28%
3 Mercedes 17%
4 Land Rover 15%
5 Porsche 11%
6 Tesla 9%
8 Aston Martin 5%
9= Honda and Lexus 3%

Most polite drivers
1 Ford 21%
2 Kia 16%
3= Volvo, Toyota, Skoda & Nissan 15%
7 Mini 14%
8 Vauxhall & VW 13%
10 Bentley 9%

43 Write offs

Having a vehicle 'written off' means being told the car was not worth repairing after an insurance claim. A recent survey of London drivers found that almost half have written off a car. A staggering 48% had seen their vehicle scrapped after an insurance claim.

44 The beautiful Beast

No apologies for writing about this thing again. I think I even mentioned it in my last car trivia book. I just love the gloriously monstrous nature of what is officially the largest car engine ever made. Find an image of it if you can – with the driver looking tiny perched on seat behind a huge bonnet containing the size of engine you'd normally find in an ocean-going liner. This 28.5-litre petrol engine was fitted to what was called the Fiat S76, nicknamed 'the Beast of Turin'.

The Beast was built in 1910 with a view to break the land speed record. The engine was bigger than most aircraft engines at the time but its limited sophistication meant it only produced around 300bhp.

The engine was connected to the wheels via heavy-duty metal chains like a hardcore motorbike. Using these the Beast was able to hit a top speed of 134mph/216kph. This was impressive for the time but not enough to set a new land speed record. The S76 was shelved after only a few trial runs because of the outbreak of the First World War.

• The biggest conventionally-powered combustion engine on earth is the poetically-named Wärtsilä-Sulzer RTA96-C. It's a rather large thing. The engine is 89 feet long, 44 feet wide and taller than most houses. If it was rated for displacement it would qualify at 25,480 litres. That's around the same size as 25,000 hatchback engines.

Its fourteen cylinders can generate an insane 107,389hp with more than 7,000,000Nm of torque.

The engine is designed to power the largest ocean-going container ships. It consumes 39 barrels of heavy fuel oil an hour (that's 1,365 gallons an hour) and costs around £22/$28 per minute to run (that's around £32,000/$40,000 a day).

45 Minor surgery

When Alec Issigonis showed his boss Lord Nuffield the design for the revolutionary new Morris Minor shortly after the Second World War, the aristocratic Morris chairman described it as 'looking like a poached egg'.

Issigonis wanted the new family saloon to feature a flat-four engine and front-wheel drive but that was too radical for Nuffield who instead insisted that the car be widened by four inches.

So the prototype was simply cut down the middle and a strip inserted - which is why there is a flat strip down the centre of the Minor's bonnet. The car was launched within a year in 1948 and became a global success.

46 Uber get-away

A hapless Michigan bank robber was caught after using the Uber app to call up a get-away car. The suspect was soon arrested in his apartment where police found incriminating evidence: the money and the note he had passed to the bank tellers demanding money.

47 Mud-plugging Porsche

Young German custom car builder Marc Gemballa has built – and sold 40 – of his extraordinary 'Marsien' off-road Porsche supercars.

Gemballa, who is just 27 years old at the time of writing, calls his creation 'an adventure supercar'. The name, rather appropriately derives from the French word for Martian.

The unique conversion starts with a standard Porsche 911 Turbo S, then tunes the engine to produce up to an insane 830hp. Standing start acceleration is cut to around 0-60mph in 2.6secs.

Gemballa then adds an active off-road suspension with the ride-height able to be raised 10 inches/250mm at the touch of a button. Other upgrades include a roll cage, titanium exhaust and carbon body.

The Marsien costs from £495,000 (US$585,000).

48 Sleepy heads

A 2023 study in America found that drivers severely under-estimate how tired they are. Many in the test rated their tiredness during a long drive as 'low' – yet closed their eyes for at least 15 seconds at times without realising.

49 Toddler at the wheel

Turkish politician and former professional bike racer Kenan Sofuglu has created a global social media following for his toddler son Zayn – by filming him driving supercars and bikes. In one of the films three-year-old Zayn is shown clambering onto a Honda Goldwing that is taller than him and riding it away. In another he is shown in a full race-suit driving a $500k red 1000bhp Ferrari SF90 Stradale V8 on a track using a booster seat, paddle shifters and pedal extensions.

Many of the Sofuglu family have motorsport careers and two of his brothers, also racers, died in bike accidents.

50 Unique Chevy

The Chevrolet Corvair was named as an amalgam of two of the manufacturer's coolest models, the Corvette and Bel Air... but it was nothing like either.

It launched in 1960 as a response to the popularity of the VW Beetle. It remains the only American-designed, mass-produced passenger car with a rear engine.

The Corvair was produced for ten years in various forms as a four-door saloon, two-door coupe, convertible, estate, van and pick-up.

At the time it was the subject of damaging rumours about the unsafe handling characteristics of a rear-engine car but a NHTSA investigation found it was no more dangerous than any other similar car. Overall Chevy sold around 1.8 million Corvairs and now it is much prized by classic car collectors.

51 GTA star

The fastest car in the latest update of the video game GTA is the Progen T20 hypercar, a creative mix of the McLaren P1 and Ferrari 488GTB. Its top speed is 122mph (197kph). Players need to pay $2,200,000 to acquire it.

52 Auto appeal

Recent research from Auto Trader website in the UK found that 12% of people think a car can make a person more attractive.

53 Insane legacy

It was sometimes described as "the most insane car ever built", but when eccentric British car builder John Dodd died aged 90 in 2022 he left his most famous creation to be auctioned.

It was an enormous 19-foot-long (5.9m) completely road-legal estate car, coloured biege. Under the huge bonnet was a world-war-two Spitfire engine, a 27-litre Rolls Royce V12. The car itself was made of featherlight fibreglass so the car was claimed to be capable of more than 200mph (300kph). It drank a gallon of fuel a minute and returned fuel economy of around 2mpg.

The extraordinary one-off vehicle was sold in March 2023 for £72,500 ($88,000).

54 Daylight robbery

Four police cars parked in front of a police station in San Francisco had their catalytic converters stolen by thieves in broad daylight in 2022. The building houses the SWAT team and bomb squad.

55 Raj Roller

In 1925 Rolls Royce produced a special one-off car for the Maharaja of Kotah Umed Singh II in India. It was an eight-litre Torpedo Sports Tourer with raised ground-clearance, massive front spotlights and finished in sumptuous black crocodile leather to be used as the Maharaja's hunting car.

It featured a built-in pistol holster, an elephant gun rack, ammunition box and had a bespoke wooden trailer holding a hand-cranked .45 caliber machine gun – for shooting tigers.

* In 2013 the Maharaja's car was auctioned in Las Vegas and sold for more than US$1 million (£810,000).

56 Half baked

The boss of a British car leasing company publicised a strange 'life hack' via an expensive PR campaign in 2023. Gavin Conway of Select Car Leasing advised UK motorists of his elaborate recommended way to remove smells from car interiors.

"There are only a few basic items you need that most people will have lying around in order to remove smells from your car. This includes two plastic Tupperware boxes and some bicarbonate soda (baking soda) - which you can find in any supermarket 'baking aisle'.

"Firstly, ensure that the plastic tupperware container is cleaned thoroughly. Once that's sparkling, grab the lid and stab a few holes on the top of it.

Then, fill half of the container with baking soda and place the lid on top. Do this twice over, so that you have two half-filled containers of baking soda with holes in the lid.

"Next, place the two containers under each front seat and leave them in the car overnight. In the morning, all bad odours should be completely gone and your car will be smelling brand new.

"If you don't have the Tupperware containers, this can be also done by pouring baking soda on areas in the car that are giving off a bad odour, however, the Tupperware method is easier, as it doesn't require you to vacuum afterwards.

"Baking soda can remove bad odours from cars because it has an absorbent structure that helps it soak up smells, and it's also a mild alkaline compound that can neutralise acidic odours.

"When you use baking soda in your car, it traps and absorbs the bad smells, and also helps to neutralise them after a number of hours."

57 Seventies sellers

UK top selling cars, 1977
1 Ford Cortina
2 Ford Escort
3 Morris Marina
4 Austin Mini
5 Austin Allegro
6 Vauxhall Chevette
7 Ford Capri
8 Vauxhall Cavalier
9 Ford Fiesta
10 Datsun Sunny
11 Sunbeam Alpine
12 Ford Granada
13 Austin Princess
14 Hillman Avenger
15 Austin Maxi
16 Datsun Cherry
17 Triumph Dolomite
18 Vauxhall Viva
19 Fiat 127
20 Fiat 131

58 Roll rocker

Motorist Mauricio Henao was just getting in his Honda saloon outside his home in Malibu, California when his girlfriend called. She asked him to go back in the house to fetch a bag she'd forgotten.

As Mauricio got back in the house he heard a huge crash. He looked outside to see a massive boulder had rolled down the hill and completely crushed his car. He told ABC reporters early in 2023 he felt so lucky to be alive that "I think I should play the Lotto now".

59 Car love

A survey in Britain in 2023 found that more than one in ten (11%) admitted to being in love with their car. Almost one in five (18%) of owners give their car a pet name.

60 Long Roller

The Rolls Royce L-Series V8 engine is one of the longest running car engines of all time.

The company introduced it as a 6.2-litre unit in 1959 to power the Silver Cloud II and Phantom. It had so much potential power and was so understressed that engineers have been able to tuned, expand and turbocharged it ever since.

It was last used in Bentley Mulsanne until 2020 having grown to a twin-turbo 6.75-litre engine.

61 Loss leaders

The latest depreciation figures in the UK show that the worst losses in values among used cars are:

1 Land Rover Discovery
2 Mini Paceman
3 Audi SQ5
4 Vauxhall Mokka
5 Tesla Model S

62 Complicated consumptions

Here's another whinge about the complexities of writing about cars. Methods of calculating car fuel consumption are strangely different all over the world.

In the US, UK and Canada it is mostly worked out on the basis of miles per gallon.

Awkwardly though, the US and UK have different sized gallons. An Imperial gallon is 4.54 litres, the US gallon is 3.78 litres.

In the rest of the Americas and Asia it's more common to calculate kilometers per litre. In the Middle East however, it is presented as kilometers per 20 litres.

63 Boxy donor

The Fiat 124 was a fairly anonymous boxy mid-range model launched in Italy in 1966 – observers at the time would be astonished to know it would go on to become one of the major cars of the 20th century.

Fiat itself built a 124 saloon, estate, coupe and convertible. But at the same time it licensed the design extensively to other manufacturers in developing nations.

In the USSR it was built as the VAZ-21011 Zhuguli which was exported with the branding of 'Lada' – and this version of the little-known Fiat alone has sold over 17 million units.

In India meanwhile, the 124 was fitted with the engine from a Nissan Sunny and sold as the Premier 118NE from 1985. Similarly in Malaysia it was the Sharikat Fiat and in Spain it was the SEAT 124. Bulgarian-built versions were called Pirin-Fiats and it was the Murat 124 in Turkey. South Korean factories used the 124 template to make Fiat-KIAs and in Egypt Lada-Egypt built at least 9,000 of its own version of the long-lasting Fiat.

Someone cleverer than me, armed with lots of facts and figures on sheets of paper has concluded that all this made the Fiat 124 the fifth best-selling car platform of all time.

• Incidentally, while it may have looked like a classic boring three-box car, the original publicity stunt to promote the launch of the 124 in 1966 was one of the most spectacular ever. It was filmed being pushed out of the back of an aeroplane. The car tumbled out into mid-air on what appeared to be a wooden pallet and then descended to the ground thanks to twin parachutes. This is before computer animation or fake videos of course.

At the same time four men in white jump suits and helmets leapt from the plane and parachuted down alongside the car. The advert showed the men land a short distance from the car, ran over to it and pull flimsy protective polystyrene panels from under the car. Then they all get in – and it starts immediately. The Fiat team then drive the new saloon off the pallet and away into the distance as the words FIAT 124 fill the screen.

64 Dangerous safety

Quoted in Autocar magazine in 2023: "Think driving at night and in bad weather conditions is the most dangerous type of driving? Think again. As writer Tom Vanderbilt says in his 2008 book Traffic "There is a simple mantra you can carry about you in traffic: When a situation feels dangerous to you, it's probably more safe than you know; when a situation feels safe, that is precisely when you should feel on guard. Most crashes… happen on dry roads, on clear, sunny days, to sober drivers.""

65 Justin time

American motorist Justin Kilmer fastidiously documents his car ownership on a YouTube channel, including all his maintenance jobs and service records.

His wife bought their 3-litre V6 Honda Accord with a manual gearbox when they were dating in 2003. Since then, Kilmer's job as a medical courier has involved covering huge mileages carrying blood, medicine and medical supplies to hospitals. This means that the standard Accord, with its original petrol engine, has now clocked up just over a million miles.

Kilmer's advice is to stick to all service schedules and replace all fluids and consumable parts as soon as necessary. His million-mile car is only on its third set of spark plugs and second clutch however. The original clutch was only replaced at 948,000 miles.

"Other than the car's achievement and sentimental attachment to having it for 20 years, countless families have been helped by having medicine/blood/supplies delivered to nursing homes, private residences, hospitals, and blood banks," Kilmer told Jalopnik.com. "That's a great legacy for this car."

66 Short-lived duo

The story of the Kaiser-Frazer Corporation was an amazing amalgamation of two proud mega-industrialists – which unsurprisingly didn't last long. Henry Kaiser, a steel baron, ship-builder and constructor of the Hoover Dam, teamed up with Joe Frazer, boss of Graham-Paige, a long-standing farm and motor engineering manufacturer.

The two men decided to join forces in 1945 and were soon churning out their new Kaiser-Frazer cars using an old wartime aircraft factory in Willow Run, Michigan. They had built 11,000 by the end of 1946 and by summer 1948 were already celebrating the 300,000th car off their production line.

That year things started to go wrong for the dynamic duo as America's Big targeted the new local upstart by launching fiercely priced rival models to the Kaiser-Frazer.

Tensions rose. Frazer warned they should scale down production, Kaiser retorted that 'Kaisers never retrench'.

It wasn't long before Frazer resigned and concentrated on making farm machinery.

Kaiser's answer was of course not to 'retrench' but to launch the Henry J saloon, a luxury sedan named after himself. A shareholder sued saying the 'ridiculous' name demonstrated 'a deep ingrained megalomanic desire for personal publicity.' The name, however, stayed.

At the same time he dropped his old partner's Frazer name from the company.

The indefatigable Kaiser bought up the old Willys Jeep utility vehicle manufacturer and battled on making Henry cars until 1955. Then he shifted production to Argentina, where they were still built until 1961. Up to that point a total of 760,000 cars had been made in nine years at the duo's Willow Run production line.

Whatever happened, Kaiser seemed to have the money-making knack. Despite the downturns, he finally sold his Argentinian operation to Ford and Renault and his 'Kaiser-Jeep' company to AMC at huge profits.

67 Motor city medium

The year of 2022 saw a series of astonishing car thefts in Detroit – right from the factories where the cars where being made.

In one evening a dozen brand new Ford Mustangs and two Jeep Wagoneers were taken from their Michigan manufacturing plants.

Similar thefts included a 'handful' of Mustang GT500s taken from their Flat Rock assembly plant, seven Chevy Camaros taken from the GM factory and $1 million worth of Ford Raptors pinched from their factory compound.

One group of youths was even caught trying to steal brand new Hellcats right from the Dodge assembly line.

68 Luxury roadtrips

A high-end holiday operator called Ultimate Driving Tours offered three-night luxury breaks to watch the 2023 Las Vegas Formula-One Grand Prix. They were priced at the top end too: from US$21,490/£17,766 per person.

The price, as much as buying a small hatchback car, included three nights at the five-star Bellagio Hotel with views over the racetrack and VIP hospitality at the first-ever Las Vegas Grand Prix including gourmet trackside catering.

69 Victory by design

Bronx-born car designer Barney Roos created new cars for Studebaker in America and then Humber, Hillman and Sunbeam in Great Britain before World War Two.

When he attended the 1937 Berlin Motor Show he inadvertently witnessed Hitler giving a speech. The speech was so vitriolic it convinced Roos that the Nazi leader would soon declare war and invade England.

So he promptly moved back to the safety of America. There he joined the Willys company. One of his first jobs was to design the Jeep – which became one of the most significant contributions to the Allied victory in the war.

70 Wild Rovers

A study of a year's worth of data showed that Range Rovers are seven times more likely to be stolen than the average vehicle in the UK.

71 The Turbo Rocket

The 1962 Oldsmobile Jetfire was a ground-breaking two-door version of the company's Cutlass saloon. It's easily spotted by its pillarless side windows.

The Jetfire was powered by a new turbocharged version of the 215 V8, immodestly called 'The Turbo-Rocket' by Oldsmobile marketing team. This engine was a breakthrough and made the Jetfire the world's first turbocharged production car.

At the time it cost $300 more than the standard Cutlass. Owners were able to monitor the performance of the new turbo via a pressure gauge on the dashboard. The suspension was the typically soft and bouncy style of the era but turbo Jetfire was much faster than the normal car. The new engine meant it could do 0-60mph in 9.2 seconds and its top speed was 110mph (176kph).

The Turbo-Rocket was impressively ahead of its time – but horrific reliability problems restricted sales to less than 4,000 cars.

72 The world's least imaginative name

When Mazda launched a people-carrying minivan in 1988 they didn't seem to have an idea for a name –they simply called it the 'Mazda MPV'.

Perhaps the marque was worried that its previous people-carrier, the Bongo, had a rather quirky name that only appealed to niche-buyers and would deter mass-market sales. The brand's new multi-purpose passenger vehicle was the latest in a wave of similar vehicles produced by global manufacturers to follow the fashion set by the pioneering people carriers like the Renault Espace.

The Mazda MPV name seemed to work. It strike a chord with buyers and sold over million units worldwide.

73 Worst product award
The excellent Jalopnik.com website nominated this bizarre item, as 'the worst automotive product for sale on the entire Amazon website' in 2023:
Gun-shaped seatbelt clips that act as defeat devices for seatbelt warning alerts. The clips also feature a built-in bottle-opener.

74 Multiple misdemeanours
In March 2023 police in Victoria, Australia, gave a traffic ticket to a woman driver for driving without a windshield, rear window, headlights, bumpers (fenders) or bonnet (hood). Her Hyundai Palisade SUV was basically a wreck that had been involved in an accident.

75 Car watchers
Around 8% of British car owners have installed CCTV to monitor their car at their home.

76 New hues
In the mid-fifties car-makers started realising the influence of general fashion trends on car choice. Soon far more automotive paint colours were being introduced in a bid to attract this more fashiona-conscious public.
DeSoto, for example, launched colours called Shell Pink, Iridescent Plum and Iridescent Lavender in 1956. That same year, Ford introduced colour options called Amethyst and Wisteria, which became very popular choice for the up-market Lincoln Premiere.
Also in 1956, Pontiac offered the paint options Camellia and Amethyst that both proved popular with women drivers.

77 Pain in the neck

Californian designer Benjamin Katz once read through a pile of police reports about traffic accidents. He noted that a large proportion of people suffered neck and spinal injuries because their head snapped backwards during collisions.

This gave him the idea to create a car head restraint system. He drew up a design for the first car seat headrest and patented it in 1921.

Sadly, it took 40 years for the idea to catch on with manufacturers.

78 Tesla troubles

Hundreds of angry car owners protested outside Telsa showrooms across China in 2023 – after the company drastically cut its prices.

Buyers who had previously paid the full price for the luxury electric vehicles were furious when prices were chopped by up to a quarter. They invaded showrooms demanding a refund. Many were shown in viral videos chanting 'Give us back our money'.

79 Car ferry tribute

After a 19-year-old crewman fell from a car ferry and drowned, the owners bought a new ship and named it after him. The new Woolwich Ferry across the Thames in London was named after tragic crewman Ben Woollacott in 2018.

80 Pedal peril

The American NHTSA road safety body estimates 16,000 accidents in the USA every year are caused by drivers pressing the accelerator pedal instead of the brake.

81 Super-failures

Online motoring writer Adam Ismail has published his list of ten failed supercar makers that deserved to do better.

They are:

10 Dome – The spectacular Dome Zero from Japan wowed the 1978 Geneva Show but never made it to production. But it does appear in games including Gran Turismo and Sega GT.

9 Lister – a Jaguar specialist built its Storm supercar in the 1990s using seven-litre Jag V12s but only built four.

8 Vector – they built the exotic-looking W8 and Lamborghini-based M12 but disappeared amid corporate in-fighting.

7 Bizzarrini – designed by a former Ferrari engineer, the gorgeous Strada 5300 coupe sold 133 times between 1964 and 1968 before the tiny Italian company went bust.

6 Cizeta – The V16T was a classic eighties wedge supercar with a 16-cylinder motor and quad pop-up headlamps. A handful were made before the company disappeared – while the car lives on in some versions of Gran Turismo.

5 Yamaha – Of course the company still exists but its OX99-11 doesn't. They built three of the F-1 derived concept with one front and one back seat but the idea was shelved.

4 Venturi – Being based in Monaco is a good start for a supercar builder but the Venturi 300 Atlantique and various other concepts failed to launch the company as an established supercar brand. Today it works in the electric Formula E race series instead.

3 Aixam – The French builder of an eccentric early monstrous crossover, powered by a Mercedes V12, failed to cut it in the supercar world. The high-riding, fire-breathing Mega Track deserved more. Now Aixam is very different – it is a manufacturer of micro electric cars.

2 Lotec – Only one of the outrageous twin-turbo 1000bhp C1000 was built by this German specialist and sold to an Arabian businessman for US$3.4m/£2.8m in 1990. I think Lotec may still be trundling along quietly but their website is all in German so I can't understand it.

1 Isdera – To buy a hand-built Isdera supercar you had to phone the company CEO personally and ask. Its eccentric series of high-powered sports cars started in 1982 and included the little-known Commendatore and Imperator. Since 2017 Isdera has partnered with Chinese WM Motors producing electric vehicles.

82 Reverse gear

Car thieves were trying to steal an historic race car in summer 2023 – but had to abandon it when they couldn't figure out how to work its fiddly gearbox.

The gang, in Melbourne, Australia, took the dark green vintage sixties Brabham BT21 Formula Three car with an unusual transmission system from a private collection.

It was soon discovered, abandoned a short distance away with a broken clutch. "I don't think they could work out how to get it started properly," said a relieved owner.

83 Oriental treasure

When a Shelby Toyota 2000GT was sold at an American auction for US$2,535,000 (£2,233,500) in 2022 it became the most expensive Japanese car ever sold.

Ironically the car is so rare today because it was also the most expensive Japanese car ever offered to American buyers when it launched in 1967. The $7,150 price was considered far too high for a Japanese car.

At the time a Corvette with a V8 engine cost $4,240 while the Toyota had a humble two-litre six-cylinder engine. The 2000GT was pricier than a Jaguar E-Type or Porsche 911 too. This meant only 62 were sold in the US.

The sophisticated car turned out to be a classic though, setting world speed-endurance records, winning races – and appearing in the James Bond film You only Live Twice (although the roof had to be sawn off to fit the 6ft 2in Sean Connery).

84 Pickford package

In the thirties, some Chevrolets came with the optional 'Mary Pickford package' for the most stylish ladies. Named after the Hollywood star of the time, this optional package added a make-up tray, illuminated mirror and make-up kit specially chosen by the star.

85 Tables with a view

In March 2023 diners eating at an up-market Victorian hotel restaurant in a World Heritage Site were shocked by hapless teenage driver. The youngster somehow lost control, mounted the pavement, over a low wall and plunged into the submerged alleyway next to the smart eatery.

The car was wedged down in the pedestrian alleyway, jammed against the restaurant windows. The Kia Picanto had to be lifted away from the hotel service passageway in the heart of Bath, England, by a crane hours later – and the 19-year-old driver was arrested on suspicion of drunk driving.

86 Guiding light

In 1900 French engineer André Michelin published the first Michelin guide, a book designed to promote tourism by car, which had rarely been done before. Michelin's plan was to help promote his fledgling tyre-making company. Both the guide – and the tyres – still exist today.

87 Screen time

The earliest cars didn't have a roof. They didn't even have windows or a windscreen. When it rained occupants would normally put up an umbrella and drive on regardless.
Drivers often wore goggles to shield their eyes.
The first windscreen/windshield didn't appear until 1904. It was made of plate glass that shattered with an impact.
It wasn't until 1919 that Ford started using safety glass. It followed a trip by Henry Ford to Paris where he met French scientist Eduard Benedictus who had developed a way to sandwich a cellulose layer between two layers of glass to prevent it splintering on impact.
Ford continued to modify the design and in 1934 introduced the first curved windscreen, previously they had always been flat glass like a normal window.

88 Leyland Torino

In 1979 British Leyland launched a sporty version of one of the dullest mid-range cars it ever built: the Austin Allegro. The two-door 'Allegro Equipe' came in silver with orange and black stripes and an orange check interior. Amazingly, these styling changes attempted to catch some of the contemporary style fashions from the contemporary smash hit US TV series Starsky and Hutch (who drove a 1976 Gran Torino).

Double page magazine adverts said: "It's now even Vroomier". It was a rather desperate attempt to jazz up the Allegro in the face of competition from more modern, sportier rivals like the new Alfa Sud, Renault 5 Gordini and VW Golf GTI. The Equipe was a two-door with the range's standard and rather dated 1750cc engine. It produced a leisurely 90bhp that meant a 0-60 'sprint' took around 13 seconds.

The British manufacturers tried their hardest with their limited budget: they fitted some new wider alloy wheels, a front spoiler and fog lamps. Inside there was a smaller steering wheel, borrowed from the Mini. The car cost £4,360 ($5,340).

Sales were predictably sluggish and to most eyes the styling wasn't a success. Some buyers were even noted peeling the stripes off the body. At the latest count there are only ten examples of the Equipe still registered on UK roads.

• Amazingly though, World War Two fighter ace and celebrity Sir Douglas Bader, who had famously lost both legs in a plane crash, contacted Leyland asking if they'd make him a one-off version of the Equipe with an automatic gearbox.

The Longbridge factory staff bent the production rules and created a unique version for the heroic Sir Douglas.

89 Tesla swap

A Tesla owner in Vancouver, Canada, got into the wrong car thinking it was his own in 2023. The Tesla App on his phone had been able to open and start the stranger's car.

The two Tesla Model 3s were the same colour and Rajesh Randev was in a hurry to collect his kids from school.

As he drove to the school Randev noticed a crack in the windscreen and called his wife to ask how it had happened.

After ten minutes he received a text from the real owner, who had been able to get into Randev's car and found his name on documents inside. He asked: "Are you driving my car?"

Randev stopped, got out and saw that the car he was driving had different style wheels to his own. The two owners agreed to meet to swap cars.

90 Drink drive deterrent

Around 350,000 drivers in the US have a breathalizer-locking device in their car. This system is usually part of a penalty following a drink-driving conviction.

It is about the size of a smartphone and fixed to the steering wheel or dashboard. The driver has to blow into a tube to demonstrate a legal blood-alcohol limit before the car will start.

91 Pilot's Phaeton

Shortly after pioneer female Pilot Amelia Earhart disappeared over the South Pacific her car did too. The 1937 Cord 812 Phaeton was dismantled and sold for parts.

American classic car enthusiasts have spent years tracing all the parts and finally have rebuilt and restored the entire car. In 2023 it became the 33rd car entered into the US National Historic Vehicle Register recording cars of important heritage value.

92 Get away with it

'Hot-wiring' a car is a method of starting it without using an ignition key, usually involving a car theft or Hollywood escape scene.

It involves connecting the wires that would complete the circuit when the key is turned on. This usually connects power to the fuel pump and ignition system. Then the bare end of the wire is touched against the wire that connects to the starter motor.

It was such an easy task in the early days of car security that cars could be hotwired from under the bonnet.

The position and colour of wiring and exact methods of connecting differ between vehicles but can usually be found on the internet. Hot wiring can generally work with any form of vehicle, even with the latest keyless ignition, immobilisers or remote starting devices.

93 Hammer lights

The headlamps in Volvo's new 2023 EX90 SUV are the most complex the company has ever devised, it claims. They are arranged in a 'Thor's Hammer' shape, inspired by the Scandinavian/Marvel mythology.

Each of the two sideways T-shape lights comprise 16 LEDs. Ten form the daytime running lights. When switching to full beam, the arrangement mechanically splits open horizontally to reveal one powerful headlight.

In addition, when owners approach their EX90 it automatically unlocks and the door handles pop out from their flush fitting to greet you. At the same time each LED of the headlights flashes in sequence before opening to reveal the full headlamp, which gives a sort of automotive blink to its owner.

94 Tractor chase

A car thief jumped into a John Deere tractor and started a bizarre low-speed car chase through the heart of a North Carolina town in 2023.

Various police vehicles tried to stop the tractor unsuccessfully and followed it at speeds "up to 20mph" (32kph) they reported.

Spike strips didn't stop the tractor so officers tried shooting the tyres. The tractor continued off-road regardless, rammed a police cruiser and its driver was eventually apprehended, only after being tasered.

95 Eccentric Egg

The Electric Egg, or 'L'Oeuf Electrique, was a city car way ahead of its time, produced by French engineer and artist Paul Arzens in 1942.

The aluminium-bodied, single-seat plexi-glass bubble car used five normal car batteries under the back seat to power to 43mph (70kph) with a range of 60 miles (100km).

Eccentric inventor Arzens also built a huge two-seater luxury streamlined cabriolet based on a Buick chassis that is now in the French National Motor Museum.

He drove the Electric Egg around Paris for 50 years until his death aged 86 in 1990.

96 Moving bridge

Absent-minded commuter Sophie Montague accidentally drove onto a ferry – thinking she was driving across a bridge. The 28-year-old Londoner posted a film on social media after realising her mistake.

It showed her stationary behind a line of vehicles. Initially she thought it was a traffic jam on a bridge across the Thames – but as it started moving she realised she had driven onto the Woolwich Ferry instead.

Sophie claimed she was just following her sat nav system. Her video was liked over 100,000 times.

97 Understated opinion

Over half of drivers (56%) prefer a car that is understated and doesn't appear attention-seeking (53% men and 59% women).

98 Invicta inclusion

After my last book a wonderfully eccentric classic car enthusiast tracked me down and insisted I include a little-known 1946 British car in my next publication.

So Mr BP, this is for you (and probably no-one else because they've stopped reading by now):

The aristocratic Invicta company had been founded by an Australian old-Etonian in leafy Surrey. He was backed by sugar tycoon Oliver Lyle and produced a series of impressively fast pre-war cars.

New company owners after the war tried to capitalise on the promise shown by the earlier cars. The Black Prince was launched featuring a badge of a medieval knight in armour (Note for American readers: the son of Edward III was a dashing warrior called 'The Black Prince').

It had a state-of-the-art twin-cam, alloy three-litre straight-six engine with triple carburettors, designed by Bentley and producing 127bhp.

Everything seemed ahead of its time: a unique continuous automatic gearbox, all-round independent suspension, cushioned subframe to increase ride comfort and sophisticated hydraulic brakes. A twin ignition system fed two spark-plugs per cylinder.

Extras were impressive for the era too: a radio, heater and four built-in hydraulically operated wheel jacks. "Designed for those who demand and appreciate the best – the world's most advanced car" said the adverts.

So far so good. But then there was the little question of the price: £3,890 ($4766). Doesn't sound much now – but at the time it was almost four times the price of a Jaguar 3.5 Mk IV and almost the same as a Bentley or Rolls.

Also the Black Prince was a little over-armoured. It was much too heavy to be spritely and that innovative gearbox was unreliable. Apart from that it arrived in a Britain reeling from the war, mired in rebuilding, rationing and austerity.

By 1949 poor old Invicta stopped trying to make or sell the thing. The total output of the Invicta Black Prince over the three years was just 16 cars.

99 Nazi paint-job

California police paid US$75,000 compensation to a motorist with Jewish ancestors in 2023 after two racist officers spray-painted a swastika on his Hyundai Elantra.

Second gear
From speed-free zones...
to severe clocking

100 Speeding hot spots
Let's start this section with yet another recent survey. This time it's the British town with the fewest annual speeding offences. Top of the least speedy area is the north eastern cathedral city of Durham, second is Derbyshire in the midlands region, third is rural Wiltshire (despite me living there at the time).
Most speeding per 1,000 residents? The eastern county of Lincolnshire (5.43 offences per 1,000 drivers).
A road safety spokesman was quoted at the end of the survey saying: "Lincolnshire is a rural county with plenty of long straight A-roads that might tempt drivers to put their foot down. But while there are few of us who can honestly say we've never bust a speed limit, the less we do it, the better."

101 Car treat
23% of car owners say they have bought their car a Christmas present in the past.

102 Salute the flag
A starting flag from the 1967 Le Mans 24-hour race sold at an American auction in 2020 for US$36,580 (£30,000). The 1967 race was the only time an all-American car, team and drivers have won.

103 Police tweets

An exasperated Police Sergeant Paul Cording tweeted this in March 2023:
"One of my team was at court in Harrogate today with a drug driver who was convicted and disqualified from driving. Unbelievely he left the courtroom and got straight behind the wheel of a car to drive home."

His next tweets:
"Officers got behind the vehicle and requested it to stop which it failed to and then drove dangerously along the A59 and north onto the A1M. Weaving dangerously in and out of traffic using the hard shoulder, the vehicle reached speeds of over 140mph.
"The vehicle then headed towards Leeming where a stinger was deployed by our ARV colleagues before being safely stopped and the driver arrested. A complete disregard for road safety and the judicial system. Driver has been charged and remanded to court in the morning."

Within 12 hours the tweet was viewed 63,200 times.

104 Drift champs

Formula D racing series is a North American driving championship where you don't have to cross the finish line first to win. The 'D' stands for 'drifting'.
The eight rounds of the championship are decided on drifting style round corners, with line and angle being more important than speed.
Current three-time champion is Norwegian stunt driver Frederic Aasbo who drives Toyotas.

105 Supercar kids

Latest data from the UK's largest track-day experience-provider shows that more than a quarter of all its bookings are for young drivers aged between ten and 16 years old.
The most popular package offered by trackdays.co.uk was for under-17s driving a trio of Aston Martin, Porsche and Ferrari supercars.

106 Hello vehicle

More than four in ten (42%) of motorists greet their cars when they walk up to it.

107 The Mopar motorcar

The Mopar brand was invented by Chrysler executives in 1937 as a combination of 'motor' and 'parts'. It was originally the brand name they used to sell Chrysler antifreeze.

Since then Mopar has become a global parts and accessory brand – and even designs and builds a small number of customised vehicles.

The best known Mopar car was the 2017 Mopar Challenger. There were 160 cars of the special limited edition can built. Half were blue, half silver.

108 Carlton's choice

Ron Carlton of Cheltenham, Gloucestershire, England, bought his Vauxhall Carlton estate "only partially because of my name.

"I wanted an estate that was big enough and there weren't many rivals. I suppose the name swung it to some degree,' he says. "I'm very happy with it but at first people did make jokes about me having the same name.

"It's worst when you go to get it serviced, they think you're not really with it because you keep saying 'Carlton' to them."

109 Drive-through peril

Changes to the UK Highway Code mean that paying for drive-through food using a mobile phone could land them a £200 fine and six points on their driving licence – for using a phone while at the wheel of a car, even if it is stationary.

110 Driving test fraud
A 29-year-old woman from Llanelli in Wales made a huge amount of money by taking more than 150 driving tests for other people.

In 2022 Inderjeet Kaur was jailed for eight months after a national police investigation found she had taken tests impersonating scores of learner drivers in South Wales, Birmingham and London. She charged the learners, who often had difficulty speaking or reading English, £800 each time.

The investigation began after a driving examiner became suspicious when Kaur arrived at the test centre just four minutes before a test and appeared completely unstressed. Kaur had the correct driver's ID documents but she didn't look anything like the ID photo.

All the drivers who passed their tests thanks to Kaur had their passes revoked.

111 Greek tragedy
Top Gear magazine reported that London psychotherapist Anne Proton is the only person in the UK with her surname. She believes it originates in Greece. She doesn't own a car but says people always make jokes about her getting… a Proton of course.

She says: "I had a look at one and I thought it doesn't look bad, actually. But I don't really know anything about cars."

112 Electric shocks
A survey of UK motorists in 2021 found that 1 in 5 'dislike electric vehicles'.

The main reasons given were:
1.   Not enough charging points
2.   Having to stop on long drives to charge up
3.   They're too expensive to buy
4.   It's too expensive to set up a charger at home
5.   I can't charge at home (no parking space)
6.   I don't trust the technology
7.   I would miss the sound of an engine

113 Two-wheeled bus

American stunt driver Bobby Ore holds the world record for driving the longest distance in a London double-decker bus on two wheels – 810 feet/247 meters.

114 Christen your car

About quarter of car-owners give their vehicle a name. Ford owners are the most likely to do this.

115 Kidnapped champion

In 1958 gunmen kidnapped the world's most famous racing driver on the eve of the Cuban Grand Prix.
Members of Fidel Castro's rebel army burst into a top Havana hotel and took Juan Manual Fangio prisoner at gunpoint.
Fangio had won the previous year and was expected to win again having set the fastest times in practice sessions.
Nevertheless, the race was held without him while all the other drivers were quickly given armed guards.
While Fangio was held prisoner in a private house he was allowed to listen to the race on a radio. The Argentine world champion was released unhurt after 29 hours.

116 Starting small

On its first-ever day of operation, in April 1915, the American Automobile Association consisted of five motorcyclists who toured St Louis looking for stranded motorists. That first Sunday they helped 24 motorists by making minor engine and tyre repairs at the roadside.

117 The car in front

The Cord L-29 was the first American front-wheel-drive car. As a car produced in Indiana it mimicked the mechanical systems of the era's top Indy racers, including lower height, inboard brakes and better rear suspension.

Launched in 1929, it won awards all over the world for its elegant design. The cockpit was very well equipped for the time, with fuel, electric, temperature, oil and speed gauges. The Cord was among America's most expensive cars of the day, costing around $3,000 (£2,400).

The Great Depression limited sales to just 4,400 though and the L-29 was discontinued within three years.

118 Go-faster camera

The Gatso speed camera system was invented by a rally driver who wanted to drive faster. Dutch motorsport star Maus Gatsonides devised the camera speed detector in 1958 to measure his cornering speed accurately and learn to go faster round bends.

119 Luxury door lights

The Lexus LS430 of 2001 was the first car to feature an illuminated doorsill. The word Lexus appeared in lights when the door was opened after dark.

120 Hamster escapes

While filming a driving challenge for BBC Top Gear in 2006 presenter Richard Hammond crashed at the wheel of a jet-powered 'Vampire' dragster at 288mph (463kph).

His front right tyre blew, swerving the car off the track onto grass. It rolled over despite the parachute braking system deploying.

The safety cage dug deep into the ground and Hammond's helmet hit the grass at speed. His head embedded itself, dislodged the visor and forcing dirt into his mouth and eye. Experts say if the famously diminutive presenter had been any taller he would have been killed.

* In an interview after his recovery Hammond revealed that he has a pact with his co-presenters in the event of them being killed in an accident. The following episode of Top Gear would open with the remaining two presenters solemnly mentioning the death and then remaining silent for a moment. They would then start a new sentence, in which the first word would be 'Anyway' and continue to happily report about cars as though nothing major had occurred.

121 Shuttle speed trial

Wealthy American dentist Dr Larry Caplin bought the first SSC Tuatara produced. Then he took it to the 2.3-mile (3.7km) space shuttle runway at Florida's Kennedy Space Centre – to see how fast it would go. Using sophisticated 'Racelogic' measuring technology the Doc clocked 295mph (475kph).

122 Road rage

Nearly three-quarters (73%) of male drivers admit that they show anger or resentment towards their car if it performs badly.

123 SOS spots

There is an emergency free phone positioned on the hard shoulder a mile apart along all UK motorways.

124 Accident prone

Maybe I should apologise for including so many of these daft surveys. They keep arriving here at Trivia Towers almost daily. But they can be interesting, like this one:

Hit comes from summer 2023 and was done by an insurance company that claims to have found the UK cities with the least risk of traffic accidents per 10,000 inhabitants.

In order of safety (and accidents per 10,000 people) they are:
1.   Aberdeen 2.78
2.   Swansea 6.60
3.   Stoke-on-Trent 7.85
4.   Dundee 7.97
5.   Cardiff 8.16
6.   Bath 9.20
7.   Glasgow 9.73
8.   Edinburgh 9.73
9.   Newport 11.09
10.   Milton Keynes 11.38

Therefore Aberdeen has way less accidents than anywhere else. In fact it only had 59 accidents in the whole year being studied. The press release from the insurance company nevertheless tells motorists this pompous bit of advice: "It's still important to stay alert while driving so that you can identify any potential hazards."

125 Fiddling with Ferraris

When Ferrari launched its new flagship four-seater, the V12-powered FF in 2011, the company wanted to outdo its luxury brand rivals in offering a huge range of extras and personal choices.

So Ferrari upgraded its customisation programme to allow clients to completely personalise their cars, right down to the style of stitching on the leather interior, the number of coats of paint, the style of door handles and the shape of exhaust tailpipe.

Ferrari set up a dedicated space at its Maranello factory to serve as its 'haute couture salon' where buyers can consult with a team of experts on creating a completely bespoke car. "Features affecting the car's performance and safety cannot be modified, neither can the fundamental design of the car, but clients can make changes to all other areas of their new Ferrari," they said. The FF cost around US$300,000/£275,000 at launch.

126 Start of motorway

Italy built the world's first motorway, the A8 heading north from Milan, in 1923.

It was the world's first purpose-built highway exclusively for motorised traffic. The German AVUS high-speed straight was earlier but was also part of a race-track and testing circuit.

Italy's motorway pioneering was extraordinary considering the entire country only had 85,000 motor vehicles of any kind at the time. Horse carts and bicycles were the more common form of Italian transport.

127 Car peep

17% of car owners regularly look outside to check their car is still there.

128 Double accelerator

The 1901 Wilson-Pilcher car was launched in Britain with a hand-controlled speed governor to control acceleration. Confusingly for drivers however, it also had a foot throttle, which could over-ride the hand control. This pedal could be pressed to increase speed – and also lifted by putting a foot under the pedal to decrease the speed.
The company ceased trading in 1904.

• Walter Wilson of the Wilson-Pilcher car company later teamed up with farm engineer William Tritton to design the first tank during World War One.

129 Black Phantom

Rolls Royce purists were shocked when eccentric carmaker Alexandre Danton recently unveiled his latest supercar – a six-wheel all-black version of the luxury Roller, the Phantom.
His matt-wrapped monster car features bull-bars, steel roof rack with spotlights and wide-wheels housed in extended wheelarches. Danton, who calls himself a 'car and sculpture artist', builds one-off motoring creations at a workshop under his chateau near Lyon, France. He plans to auction the six-wheeled Rolls creation for £4.3million/$5.2million.

130 Smoking fine

Although the act of smoking whilst driving in the UK is not illegal, motorists who are distracted behind the wheel whilst smoking could be fined £100 for careless driving with three points on their licence.
It is definitely against the law, however, to smoke in the car whilst carrying passengers under the age of 18 - this ban was introduced in 2015 to protect younger ones from second-hand smoke.

131 Marque magic

About two thirds of all motorists admit they would never buy certain car brands simply because of their built-in snobbery about some car badges.

132 Luxury bus
The latest Dembell luxury motorhome is so big it includes a portable garage big enough to hold a Ferrari. The triple-axle German land-yacht is the size of a bus and costs over a million Euros/dollars/pounds.

133 Jam centres
A recent global survey of 1,000 cities found the most congested roads in the world are in London. The A219 in South London was named the worst road in the city for delays. Runners-up were Chicago, Paris, Boston and New York.

134 Theft total
Almost a million cars are stolen a year in the US.

135 One shop
The Mercedes One supercar uses a combination of petrol and electric power to accelerate from 0-60mph in 2.9 seconds. Top speed is limited to 219mph/352kph but it could go faster. Average fuel consumption is 27mpg.
It launched in 2022 and prices started at US$3 million/£2.5m – but you needed to travel to Germany to buy one. It is only sold from the Mercedes head office in Stuttgart.

136 Turbine racer

The 51st Indy 500 in 1967 was dominated by former stock-car racer Parnelli Jones. He was driving a revolutionary new car – the STP-Paxton Turbocar gas turbine.

This had four-wheel drive, aluminium 'backbone' frame and turboprop aircraft engine. The driver sat to the righthand side of the backbone, the engine on the left.

Jones agreed to drive the pioneering car after being given $100,000 in cash in a briefcase and promised half of any prize money.

He started at sixth place on the grid but passed four cars before the first turn and was leading by turn two. His first lap was a record 154mph and he opened up a sizeable lead over the rest of the field. With four laps to go he was over a lap ahead of the nearest car.

Suddenly a minor component – a transmission bearing costing $6 – failed and the car simply coasted to a halt. Eventually A.J Foyt sailed past and won the race.

* The car was repaired and entered into the 1968 Indy 500 driven by Joe Leonard. He crashed into the wall on turn four during a practice session and the car never appeared again.

137 Rude roads

I recently received a press release from a car leasing company that had decided it would be informative/hilarious to compile a roadtrip around the UK streets with the rudest names. These people really don't have much to do they? Anyway, here is what they came up with:

"From Backside Lane to Crotch Crescent, motoring experts at LeaseCar.uk have researched the UK's most offensive road signs to create the ultimate route for cheeky travellers.

Despite its prim and proper reputation, the UK is littered with smutty-sounding signs, meaning the rude road trip takes in all four corners of the country.

Shrewsbury, Doncaster and Edinburgh are just three areas drivers will tick off as they embark on the road trip to hunt down UKs crudest spots. And as motorists make their way along the glorious south coast, enjoying the beautiful beach views of St Ives, they can grab a selfie with the infamous Court Cocking road sign. Wales also has a few corkers, with Fanny Street in Cardiff causing many an eyebrow to raise as road trippers drive by.

Some road names, like Bell End in Rowley Regis, are so outrageous that they have devalued homes in the area and allegedly caused humiliation and bullying for residents. Research shows that innuendo-laden roads have an average 22% dip in price compared to other houses in conventionally named streets nearby.

This is bad news for many homeowners because there are at least 17 Cock Lanes across England and Wales. However, despite petitions by local residents to try and change the inappropriate names, councils report having no plans to do so which is excellent news for those eager to make this road trip.

Tim Alcock at Leasecar.uk said: "This country is known for its eccentric nature, and the general reaction to these wacky road names really demonstrates our frank British humour. We have created the rudest road trip in the UK, which is bound to be the weirdest drive you'll ever take.

"From Dick Place in Edinburgh and Semicock road in Northern Ireland, this road trip is so inappropriate we suggest not taking your kids on this one.

"Who knows how long these roads will keep their rude names as we're already seeing residents want to get them changed. Have a laugh and visit these crude spots across the UK as soon as you can before they just become a part of history."

Here is Leasecar.uk's rudest road trip in the UK:
- Backside Lane, Doncaster, South Yorkshire
- Dick Place, Edinburgh, Scotland
- Assloss Road, Kilmarnock, Scotland
- Semicock Road, Ballymoney, Northern Ireland
- Trailcock Road, Carrickfergus, Northern Ireland
- Slack Bottom, Hebden Bridge, West Yorkshire
- Lickers Lane, Prescot, Lancashire
- Spanker Lane, Belpher, Derbyshire
- Grope Lane, Shrewsbury, Shropshire
- Hardon Road Wolverhampton, West Midlands
- Minge Lane, Upton-upon-Severn, Worcestershire
- Fanny Street, Cardiff, Wales
- Court Cocking, St. Ives, Cornwall
- Slaparse Lane, Exeter, Devon
- Cock-A-Dobby, Sandhurst, Berkshire
- Crotch Crescent, Oxford, Oxfordshire
- Titty Ho, Raunds, Northamptonshire
- Hooker Road, Norwich, Norfolk
- Butthole Lane, Shepshed, Leicestershire
- Willey Lane, Newthorpe, Nottinghamshire

138 Parking pattern
Residents in a Melbourne suburb were outraged when council workmen lazily repaved a street recently – because they had left all the places where cars were parked untarmacked. The strange resulting curves of tarmac and bare parking spaces made the street look very strange and locals complained the work was a complete waste of money.

139 Road count
Italian aristocrat Piero Puricelli, Count of Lomnago and Fascist Senator, was also an acclaimed road engineer who designed and built the world's first motorway and the Monza race track in the 1920s.

140 Ambulance eccentric

American businessman Andy Granatelli was the ultra eccentric boss of auto oil and additive producer STP.

During the Second World War he held morale-boosting auto events for the public. These involved stunt drivers executing spectacular roll-over and end-over-end crashes. During the finale an 'ambulance' would join in a race of all the competitors and eject a stretcher into the path of the other cars as the ultimate crowd-pleaser. The stretcher's occupant was a dummy figure meant to make the crowd think a real patient was being run over.

Texan multi-millionaire Granatelli was also famous for attending every Indy 500 race from 1946 until his death from heart failure in 2013.

141 Canadian war effort

Canadian factories produced more than 850,000 vehicles during the Second World War, mostly trucks and light car-based vehicles. These were built by Ford, GM and Chrysler in their factories north of the border for use by the Allies.

142 Advanced gears

In the 1930s many cars came with a pre-selector gearbox. In this system drivers could choose their next gear before actually changing into it. At the required moment the driver could press the 'gear-change pedal' and the car automatically changed into the gear that had been chosen previously.

The pre-selector gearbox appeared in many models of the period including cars made by Cord, Daimler, Armstrong Siddeley, Talbot, ERA and Maybach. It was also later used in the World War Two German Tiger Tank.

143 Speed camera defence
The most common excuses used in UK courts to get off speeding charges:
- the cameras were faulty
- the paperwork contains incorrect details
- the speed restriction signs were missing or obscured
- the penalty notice was issued too late
- the car in question was using a false number plate

144 Toyota accidents
Between 2000 and 2010 it is believed 89 fatal accidents took place in America apparently caused by accelerator malfunction in Toyota and Lexus cars.
Safety officials spent years investigating and Toyota claimed there could be no way that its cars would unintentionally accelerate.
The breakthrough came in 2008 when it was discovered that the driver's side trim could come a little loose and prevent the accelerator pedal for returning up to its 'off' position. Further investigations found Toyota floor mats could come also loose and obstruct the accelerator pedal. The mat could even cause vehicles to suddenly accelerate without warning.
Officials believed the manufacturer had known about the problems but continued to sell the defective cars. In 2014 the US Department of Justice fined Toyota US $1.2 billion in penalties to do with the cases.

145 Core offence
A woman farmer took revenge after a three-week fling ended – she stuffed apples up the exhaust pipe of her former lover's car. Later in court the young farmer from Cheshire, England, admitted causing criminal damage.

146 Missing models

Here are the figures showing the cars most likely to be stolen in the UK with the number stolen in 2021:

1 Ford Fiesta (3,909)
2 Range Rover (3,754)
3 Ford Focus (1,912)
4 VW Golf (1,755)
5 Mercedes C-Class (1,474)
6 BMW 3-Series (1,464)
7 Land Rover Discovery (1,260)
8 Vauxhall Corsa (1,218)
9 Vauxhall Astra (1,096)
10 Mercedes E-Class (818)

147 Racing curse

The Andretti Curse is legendary sequence of bad luck befalling the Andretti motor racing family. The curse is said to have followed an incident in 1969 when family head Mario Andretti won the Indy 500.
Colourful Texan businessman Andy Granatelli (see item 140) excitedly ran to the victory lane and exuberantly kissed Andretti on the cheek. Following the kiss, says the myth, Mario never won the race again in 25 years of trying.
None of his sons Michael and Jeff, nephew John and grandson Marco managed to win it either in more than 60 years, in a series of mechanical breakdowns, crashes and last-lap disasters totalling 78 different race starts.
Some have speculated the curse was cast during an argument among the Andretti back-room team following the 1969 victory in which the wife of one of the owners said the Andrettis would never win the Indy 500 again.

148 Four trios

The Big Three is a term first used to describe America's three major car-makers:
Ford, General Motors and Chrysler (now Stellantis).
It is also commonly used in other countries too.
In Japan it refers to Toyota, Nissan and Honda.
In Germany it means Volkswagen, Mercedes and BMW.
In France the big three are Renault, Peugeot and Citroen.

149 Car theft film

CCTV footage from a dealership showroom in Kentucky, USA, in 2023 showed a slick gang of seven car thieves stealing six Challenger Hellcats from the showroom... in 40 seconds.
Each cars normally sells for around $95,000 (£78,000). Five were recovered very quickly. One was a write-off however and two others were badly damaged.
The footage of thieves stealing the six sports cars from a Kentucky dealership is still available on You Tube.

150 Colour peril

Yet another survey, this time about 'the most dangerous car colours'. This has been done before and I'm sorry I think I put a previous survey about it in my last book. But the surveys are always changing.

This one in Spring 2023 revealed the following pieces of 'research':

According to motoring safety experts at Road Angel (retailer of dash cameras) motorists who own a red vehicle are most likely to be in danger on the roads.

Research has revealed that a staggering 60% of red cars have reportedly been in accidents, making it the most dangerous colour vehicle to drive.

The shade is strongly associated with danger, and men are 12% more likely to prefer a red car than women.

Coupled with the fact that a high proportion of sports cars are red, which are manufactured for speed, it makes sense why the colour choice is so risky.

The next most dangerous car colour is brown, where 59% of car owners have reportedly been in an accident. Motorists with a black car should also be extremely cautious, as 57% of drivers with the car colour have reported incidents.

Black is the second most popular car colour. For both black and brown cars, visibility seems to contribute to why so many accidents were reported.

Owners of darker coloured vehicles could sometimes pay a higher insurance premium as insurers factor visibility into their calculations of likelihood of having an accident.

Darker colours make it harder for them to be seen on the roads, especially at night, and they also blend more into the surroundings than other shades.

For this reason, white is one of the safer colours cars to purchase as the shade makes vehicles highly visible and easy to spot on the roads.

Gary Digva from Road Angel then gave us this earth-shattering conclusion: "Buying a red car doesn't mean you will definitely get into an accident. Buying a white car doesn't mean you are invincible on the roads. Drivers should always be cautious when behind the wheel."

151 Extended dream

The world's longest car is a customised creation called 'The American Dream'. It is more than 100ft (30.5m) long and can seat more than 75 people.

It includes its own swimming pool, diving board, Jacuzzi, bathtub and mini-golf course. There is also room for a functional helipad.

The original was built in California in 1986 using a series of Cadillac Eldorados, with 26 wheels, and powered by two V8 engines, one at each end.

Recently the creator, Jay Ohrberg, a custom car designer, increased the Dream's length to 100ft – with a hinge system in the middle to allow the vehicle to get around a corner.

152 Spot control

Surveying 2,000 adults, Spotify research found that 3 in 5 motorists (57%) now believe it's the driver who should get to control the music during a roadtrip, rather than front-seat passenger or, worse, back-seat drivers.

153 Motorists' habits

The survey of UK drivers by an insurance company in 2023 found the nation's top 10 'quirky' driving habits are:

47% ensure their windscreen wipers are in the resting position before turning the engine off;

42% search out the cause of an interior noises or rattle straight-away;

39% stop the fuel pump on a round number; and an additional 39% avoid parking next to another vehicle in a car park;

35% straighten the steering and car wheels when parking;

31% ensure their fuel gauge does not drop below a designated point;

23% move to the inside lane at a specific point prior to exiting a motorway (for example, when seeing the first exit sign)

20% yell at other drivers safe in the knowledge they can't be heard;

18% avoid cat's eyes when changing motorway lanes;

17% talk to themselves in the car;

15% change gears in sequence and never skip a gear, eg changing from fourth to second gear.

Other strange things drivers do is allowing indicators to click a certain number of times before switching them off (3%). And finally almost one in ten (9%) will also avoid parking next to a specific vehicle brand of car.

154 Vanguard's voyage

After the Second World War motor manufacturers had an idea to sell cars to all the millions in the British Commonwealth who had served in navy or merchant ships.

So they named a car the Standard Vanguard after a battleship that was famously launched at the end of the war. HMS Vanguard was the Royal Navy's last ever battleship and the Standard Motor Company had extended negotiations with naval bureaucrats to be able to use the name.

HMS Vanguard was launched in 1944 and was headline news as it transported King George on the first ever royal visit to South Africa in 1947. It was soon outdated however and was sold for scrap in 1960.

The 2.1-litre Vanguard car lasted slightly longer than the ship, being produced from 1948 to 1963. The distinctive curvy design appeared in saloon, convertible, van, estate and pick-up formats in the UK, Australia, New Zealand and some parts of Europe.

A 1949 road test clocked the Vanguard's top speed as 79mph (127kph) with a 0-60 time of 21.5 seconds. Unusually for the time a diesel variant was produced too, using the engine from the sister company's Ferguson tractor. A 1954 test showed why diesel was not very popular. Top speed was just 66mph (107kph) and 0-60 time was a yawning 32 seconds. Fuel consumption of 38mpg was little compensation.

The Standard company, which also produced Triumph cars, was bought by Leyland Motors in 1960 for £20 million. After 60 years of making and selling Standards, the brand name disappeared in 1963.

In 2019 it was bought by a Florida car museum that rebuilt, renovated and enlarged the car by a further inch and a half. It was also fitted with six American flags along the massive bonnet.

155 From racing to wine

French Formula One racing driver Jean Alesi retired from racing… for a rather more quiet life, running his own vineyard near his hometown of Avignon, where he lives with his wife, former Japanese music idol Kumiko Goto.

156 Heat problem

According to various academic studies, a driver's reactions are 20% slower when the temperature in the passenger compartment exceeds 35° C (95F) compared to 25° C (77F). That is equivalent having a blood alcohol level of 0.5 grams of alcohol per litre.

157 Alpine Bond

In the first 007 film, Dr No in 1962, James Bond's first car was the modest Sunbeam Alpine Series II, in lake blue.

After being invited to the mountain apartment of an enemy spy called 'Miss Tarot', Bond drove the Sunbeam up a dusty road and right into a trap. This ended with him being chased by a funeral large hearse full of baddies that tried to ram him off a cliff. After some tense corners, the Alpine rounded a bend to find the crane blocked the road ahead. Bond managed to drive right underneath – but the hearse was too tall and skidded off the mountain to a classic fiery demise.

Like many Bond cars to follow, the Sunbeam was English-made. It was manufactured just outside Coventry in the West Midlands.

In the original Dr No book by Ian Fleming the Sunbeam was the personal car of a certain John Strangways, head of Station J, Jamaica. For the film it became Bond's own car.

Back then Bond films were not such big budget productions. For Dr No the producers had to borrow the Alpine from a local resident to avoid the cost of importing their own.

158 Geographical points

West Yorkshire drivers are the most dangerous in the UK. That is the finding of a 2023 survey matching penalty points on driving licences with geographical postcodes.

In fact the four highest scoring areas were all in West Yorkshire: Calderdale, Kirklees, Bradford and Leeds. Almost one-in-ten drivers have points on their licenses here.

The areas with the lowest number of points on the average driver's license are the remote fringes of the UK: the Shetland Isles, Isles of Scilly and the Orkney Islands where only two per cent of drivers have any points at all.

• Another 2023 survey found that the cheapest UK cities to own a car are, in order:
1 Durham
2 Stoke on Trent
3 Inverness
4 Lancaster
5 Preston
6 Stirling
7 Sheffield
8 Hereford
9 Wakefield
10 Hull
(It's all based on things like price of fuel, cost of parking and insurance ratings.)

And the priciest places to own a car?
Here goes: 1 Westminster, 2 rest of London, 3 Brighton, 4 Winchester, 5 Chelmsford, 6 Canterbury, 7 Cambridge, 8 Oxford, 9 Bath, 10 Southampton.

159 TikTok transport

And yet another 'survey' done in the name of advertising. This time an agency studied follower counts and hashtag analysis on TikTok to find the world's most popular car brands in 2023…

The results were:
1 BMW, 2 Ford, 3 Honda, 4 Audi and 5 Tesla.

160 Rolls pearl

Probably the most expensive car ever built was unveiled at a motor show on the glamorous shores of Lake Como in Italy. The second in a special series of Rolls Royce Boat Tail models came with a cool US$30m (£25m) price tag.

The hand-built four-seater convertible has individually crafted body panels of pearl oyster-coloured shimmering aluminium, bespoke walnut interior surfaces inlaid with rose-gold accents, mother-of-pearl dials… and a built-in picnic area. This is a twin-trunk arrangement that open to reveal a pop-up sunshade and colour co-ordinated crockery.

The car was already sold to an un-named businessman whose fortune derived from pearl fishing.

161 Old slogans

Random selection of old car sales slogans:

Ford Capri, the car you always promised yourself
MGTF: Safety Fast (1953)
They'll know you've arrived when you drive up in an Edsel (1958)
Chevrolet Corvette: Chevy puts the purr in performance (1957)
Morris Minor: It's one of the family now (1950s)

162 VW Seatle

Volkswagen created a new product on wheels in 2022 – a motorised office chair. The chair comes complete with an electric motor, headlights and a horn. The concept chair is available for test-drives to gauge public reactions while VW decide whether to launch it on the market.

163 Family car

One of the most successful British sports cars of the inter-war period was the Riley Nine, which sold well between 1926 and 1938. It was a remarkable one-family creation.

The factory was founded by William Riley and his son Percy Riley designed the engine, leaving his younger brother Stanley to design the chassis, suspension and body.

164 Pulling over peril

Advanced driver, Frank Wallington, 76, from Walsall, England, was driving home from a funeral when an emergency ambulance appeared behind him.

Frank cautiously pulled out of the way to let the blue flashing lights pass safely but in doing so the front end of his car slightly crossed the white line under a red traffic light.

An automatic camera caught this and the pensioner was promptly sent a £100 fine – his first-ever driving infringement.

"I'm being punished for doing the right thing," Frank told journalists.

165 Stunt disasters

Some of the worst movie car stunt accidents ever:

'Manslaughter' 1922 (film name, not the verdict)
Stunt driver Leo Noomis had to crash a police motorcycle into
the side of a car at 45 mph (72kph). It all went horribly wrong…
and Noomis broke his pelvis and six ribs.

The Warrens of Virginia 1924
Actress Martha Mansfield died when a discarded match ignited
her period costume of hoop skirts and ruffles while she sat
relaxing in a car off-set. Her chauffeur was badly injured trying
to save her.

The Horror of Party Beach 1964
Local bikers were used for a gang scene but they tried to show
off in front of the cameras, went too fast, collided with a
leading actor and triggered a pile-up with multiple injuries. As a
final blow, a police car rushing to help crashed on the way.

Pontiac commercial 1967
A camerman and an actress were killed in a brand new
Pontiac when a boom camera hanging from an on-coming car
crashed through their windscreen.

The Golden Squadron 1973
An actor and two technicians died filming this TV mini-series
when their car flew off the road into a ravine. The actor was
Roger Delgado, known for his portrayal of The Master in
BBC's Doctor Who.

No Deposit, No Return 1976
Leading stuntman Dale Van Sickel was supposed to skid off a
pier into the water but the skid went wrong and he hit a wall
instead. Van Sickel was disabled for life and his family
eventually won a large but undisclosed financial settlement
from the film-makers Disney.

The Omen 1976
The film was supposedly cursed: Gregory Peck almost severed another actor's fingers by accidentally slamming them in a car door, and team members suffered accidents in later films, including a stuntman seriously injured in a fall and a technical assistant dying in a car crash off-set.

Charlie's Angels 1979
Two stunt actresses were scripted to jump from a moving car but the driver, allegedly high on cocaine, drove insanely fast and both were badly injured.

Chips 1979
Star Erik Estrada crashed his police bike, was hurled into a park car… and then the bike landed on top of him. The actor suffered multiple fractures and collapsed lungs.

That's Incredible! 1980
The TV show's resident stunt biker Steve Lewis was badly injured trying to jump over two cars speeding towards him at more than 100mph (160kph).
Then stunt rider Gary Wells tried to jump 170 feet (52m) over the fountains at Caesar's Palace, Las Vegas, but missed the landing ramp completely and crashed into a wall. He suffered severe injuries and the wall collapsed, injuring six spectators.

The Cannonball Run 1981
Stuntwoman Heidi von Beltz was left severely disabled after being thrown from a car during a crash scene.

The Five of Me 1981
An out-of-control driverless stunt car hit a cameraman on this TV film. He died later.

Bladerunner 1982
Actress Daryl Hannah broke her elbow when she slipped on the distinctive wet shiny pavement and fell into the window of a parked car.

Midnite Spares 1983
A technician was killed during a race scene when a car swerved off the track, hitting him so hard his body flew through two fences.

Peterborough Jump 1983
A Canadian TV stuntman died when his rocket-powered Pontiac Firebird tried to jump over a pond. It overshot the landing ramp and landed on its roof.

Police Story 1985
Unusually this mishap made it into the film: Jackie Chan abruptly stops a double-decker bus and the passengers are thrown out of the upstairs window. They are supposed to land on a car – but missed and landed on the hard road surface instead. The director thought it looked so realistic the scene was used uncut.

The Wraith 1986
A sci-fi movie cameraman was killed when the overloaded filming car swerved off an Arizona mountain road while shooting a car chase scene.

The Squeeze 1987
An experienced veteran stuntman was trapped in a car and drowned after plunging off a pier into the Hudson River.

Seven 1995
Star Brad Pitt was chasing a fugitive, fell and his arm plunged right through a car windshield. He needed surgery and had to continue filming with his arm in a cast. The incident was written into the script to explain his arm cast, as if it was deliberate.

Blues Brothers 2000
A stunt car somehow rolled over onto two crew members, one of whom lost his leg. Later a stunt driver was severely injured during a mock car crash.

Kill Bill: Volume 2 2004
Star Uma Thurman suffered concussion and injured knees when she accidentally drove straight into a palm tree during a scene in Mexico.

The Dark Knight 2008
A movie cameraman was killed while filming from the back of a pickup truck driving alongside a stunt car. The stunt car turned sharply but the pickup didn't and crashed right into a tree.

Wetten, dass? 2010
Tragedy hit this popular German TV show when a stuntman attempted to use spring stilts to bounce over a sequence of five cars driving towards him. He failed to clear the fourth car (driven by his father) and hit the ground head-first, leaving him severely disabled.

Transformers: Dark of the Moon 2011
A movie extra received an $18 million settlement after suffering very serious life-changing injuries when a steel tow-rope snapped. In the scene, the rope was pulling her car behind another. When the rope broke, it flew back, hitting her car. Old footage from a previous film was used instead of the accident scene.

Nitro Circus: The Movie 2012
This 3D film was a commercial disaster and rated only a paltry 6% approval on ratings site Rotten Tomatoes. Even worse, actor and pro mountain biker Jim DeChamp broke his back in a car stunt that went disastrously wrong.

Maze Runner: The Death Cure 2018
Star Dylan O'Brien was run over by a car in a scene that went hopelessly wrong. His multiple injuries were so severe filming stopped for almost a year to allow him to recover.

LA's Finest 2019
The creator and producer of this popular TV series was seriously injured on a Los Angeles dockside when a stunt car being pulled by a cable crashed into the production team. Brandon Sonnier was watching the actual stunt on a monitor screen when the car he was watching crashed into a steel shipping container – which then toppled on to his leg. His leg had to be amputated.

Street Outlaws: Fastest in America 2022
Star Ryan Fellows was killed when his Datsun 240Z flipped over and caught fire while filming a race scene for the long-running TV show.

166 Lambo extras
The exotic Lamborghini Aventador LP 700-4 of 2011 was not only a breathtaking all-wheel drive sports car, its over-the-top factory options included a see-through bonnet, dull matt body paint and a choice of three colours for the brake calipers.

167 Shades peril
Firefighters in England's Midlands issued a warning to all motorists, everywhere, after attending a blaze that destroyed a parked car in Nuthall in 2023. It had been caused by a pair of sunglasses left in the car. They had magnified sunlight onto the dashboard and set it alight.

168 Duck tribute
When a driver stopped and got out to help shepherd a family of ducks waddle across a road in California, he was tragically hit by another motorist and died. A roadside shrine appeared at the spot near Sacremento as passers-by left flowers and toy rubber ducks in tribute.

169 Royal fleet
Petrolhead King Abdullah of Jordan's collection of cars includes vehicles worth many millions, including a 2005 Bugatti Veyron, pristine 1954 Rolls Royce Phantom IV, 1964 Aston Martin DB5, 2003 Porsche Carrera GT and 2009 Mercedes SLR Stirling Moss.

170 Tapping the market
Entrepreneur Charlie Mullins established the UK's best-known plumbing firm and spent £1.5m on personalised number plates for its fleet of vans. They include MET3R, BAS1N, 51NKS and DRA1N.

171 Forgotten supercar
In the sixties Iso Rivolta was a glamorous brand of Italian sports car. Stars of the era loved them. French singer Johnny Hallyday had an ISO A3, John Lennon and actor Alain Delon had an Iso Fidia, and the Aga Khan had a Rivolta GT.
The brand still exists and launched a Rivolta GTZ supercar in 2021, based on a Corvette.

172 Body check
Danish drivers are supposed by law to check for bodies under their car before driving off in case children are sleeping underneath.

173 Wooden world
The new 'World of Volvo' visitor centre is being built in Gothenburg, Sweden, designed around three giant wooden tree trunks. The centre will house a collection of classic Volvos and historic exhibitions – but will be built of wood and set in a landscaped plot full of wildflowers.

174 Final plans

Wealthy Australian entrepreneur Philip Allen has arranged to be buried in his favourite car when he dies.

Allen chose his 2008 Morgan Aeromax, one of only 100 ever made. The car was previously owned by Top Gear's Richard Hammond.

Allen says the detailed funeral plans have been made with the burial costing about Au$75,000 (£40k/US $50k).

"I love this car so much I've already made plans to be get buried in it, " he says. "The car will be pushed into a 20ft container, which I've already purchased, and put on jacks because I don't want the tyres to go flat.

"Then the container will be welded up so it's air- and water-tight. We dig a hole and bury it and put a concrete slab over the top to seal it off.

"I'll be partly mummified and dressed in my crocodile skin jacket, pants and boots. One hand on the steering wheel the other holding a cigar and a smile."

175 Loud and proud

The 2021 McMurtry Speirling single-seat supercar holds the unlikely title of the world's loudest electric car. It uses a massive fan system to produce downforce to hold the rear end of the road at high speeds. This enables the car to corner at enormous speeds but also produces 120 decibels – that's 30db over the normal legal limit for the noise of any new car.

176 Unwanted gift
Bianca Fitzsimmons, from Newcastle, New South Wales, Austalia, proudly posed for photos in a Ford dealership before buying her first new car. The 26-year–old was photographed next to the $77,000 Ford Ranger, which was wrapped up by the showroom staff like a gift in a fabric cover tied with a huge blue ribbon.

But within a few weeks Bianca was threatening to protest outside the dealership. She was demanding a replacement vehicle after the brand new truck developed an electrical fault in the impact collision system. This made the Ford suddenly perform emergency stops while she was driving along at 80kph/50mph.

"We apologise for the inconvenience," a Ford spokesman told journalists.

177 Company torpedoed
The Tucker Torpedo was a striking and innovative car launched in 1947 by eccentric entrepreneur Preston Tucker. Within a year however his company went bankrupt after a damning series of negative headlines about fraud in his company that were later found to be baseless. Tucker claimed the bad publicity was part of a secret campaign by the Mid-West's big three automakers to discredit him,

178 Smart traffic

Melbourne in Australia now claims to have the world's smartest traffic management system. The Victoria Department of Transport teamed with the University of Melbourne to install a massive data management system to control everything from traffic lights to bus timetables.

The computerised AI network uses thousands of CCTV cameras, Bluetooth sensors, air quality monitors, live public transport data, TomTom live traffic information, weather readings, and crossroad congestion reports.

It means all traffic light timings and lane guidance alerts constantly adapt to conditions. Trams can be automatically diverted to avoid jams, emergency vehicles can be given an immediate 'green light' corridor and traffic can be routed away from schools at drop-off and collection time. Some cars with advanced communication systems can even receive information from the city management system warning of incidents or dangers.

179 Hot lollipops

Some British road crossing attendants hold long prominent 'stop' signs on a pole to alert traffic. They are familiarly known as 'lollipops'. In some parts of Britain they have been fitted with a heated hand-grip. A special rechargeable strip embedded in the stick comes with a temperature dial, which can be adjusted depending on the weather.

180 Walker can drive

Office worker Jason Walker from Crawley, Sussex, UK – who failed his driving test 11 times and wrote off his instructor's car by hitting a lamppost at speed while practising a three-point turn – finally passed in 2006.

181 Hey you!

Over a third of drivers (34%) would challenge a thief trying to steal their car (men 43%, women 25%).

182 Art hotel

A fake hotel has been built alongside an Australia motorway. The Hotel EastLink looks like a modern multi-storey hotel but is in fact an art sculpture with no rooms at all.

The ten-storey steel and concrete building cost Aus$1.2m/£655,000 to create on the outskirts of Melbourne. There's a big red sign saying 'hotel' and some windows have lights that come on at night. It was the work of Canadian artist Callum Morton in 2007 who describes it as "a giant folly".

Not surprisingly, unwitting motorists try to stop and book rooms at 'the hotel'.

183 Four-wheel deride

More than one in five of 4X4 drivers have been in an argument with traffic wardens – compared with only six per cent of people who drive saloon cars.

184 Show-off caught

A speeding teenaged biker was caught after he posted a FOUR-PART video series of his escape from police on TikTok. He hadn't thought that the helmet-cam footage showed he was riding a very rare 2022 sports motorbike. Georgia police in the US were able to track the biker down from that information – and charge him with 13 different traffic violations.

185 Shadow's demise

Poor SYD 724F, a classic seventies white Rolls Royce Silver Shadow that suffered a long and tortured fall from grace.

First Britpop band Oasis spent £100,000 buying the luxury Rolls, purely to photograph it floating in the swimming pool of a grand country mansion. The stunt was used to take a photo for the cover of the band's 1997 album 'Be Here Now'.

The drowned limo was in such a bad state afterwards it had to be sold off to a banger-racing outfit called Team Goldilocks. The former prestige saloon was crudely sprayed red and black and fitted with a new engine – humiliatingly from a Ford Granada.

Then the Rolls was driven in a big banger race meeting in Essex in 2003. Perhaps inevitably, all the other banger drivers were very keen to deliberately crash into it. The once-luxurious Rolls Royce Silver Shadow was completely destroyed in by the collisions during the race.

186 Autonomous pile-up

A self-driving Tesla Model S abruptly stopped without warning on the San Francisco Bay Bridge in California – and caused an eight-vehicle pile up.

The crash came just hours after company boss Elon Musk had announced the launch of Tesla's 'full self-driving' capability in 2023.

Nine people, including a two-year-old child, were injured after the electric car's owner switched to the new self-driving mode and it opted to suddenly brake on the multi-lane highway while travelling at speed in heavy traffic.

187 Delivery desires

A poll among delivery drivers in 2023 found the UK roads they most liked.

- A9 – Perth to Inverness, Scotland
- A39 – The Atlantic Highway, Cornwall, England
- A55 – North Wales Expressway, Wales
- A38 – Devon Expressway, England
- A5 – London to Holyhead Trunk Road, England/Wales

And the ones they hated most:

- M6 – Birmingham to Manchester, England
- M25 – London, England
- M62 – Leeds to Manchester, England
- A13 – London, England
- A19 – Newcastle to Doncaster, England

188 Thief magnet

13% of motorists worry about buying a car that would be attractive to car thieves.

189 Mini luxuries

In the sixties the Beatles were the world's biggest pop stars. At the time they weren't supercar lovers and by the standards of today's celebrities their tastes were relatively restrained.
So they are often associated with rather humble cars. For example, all four of them owned customised Minis supplied by specialist coachbuilder Radford, based in Kensington, London. Beatles legend says that they were all gifts from their manager Brian Epstein.

John Lennon who disliked driving and rarely took to the wheel, had a black Mini Cooper S with black wheels and blacked-out windows. The car has been the object of many myths and legends. Fans have tried to track it down and some collectors claim to have it in secret storage.
John was no car enthusiast but seemed to like Minis. He bought his wife Cynthia one in 1964 after she passed her driving test and in 1971 he gave his cleaning lady a white Mini.

George Harrison had a metallic black Mini Cooper S later painted flower-power psychedelic colours that was featured in the film Magical Mystery Tour. George and John had their first LSD trip while driving in the Mini after a friend slipped it into their tea. George recalled being scared and driving very slowly. He later gave the car to Eric Clapton.

Paul McCartney had a sage green metallic Mini Cooper customised for some reason with Aston Martin light units, black leather interior and sunroof. Paul was driving the car on the first night he met Linda and drove her and singer Lulu back to his house in it.
The Mini still exists: it was sold in the USA in 1996 and now on display at the Sarasota Classic Car Museum in Florida beside John Lennon's Mercedes.

Ringo Starr had a maroon Mini Cooper that was made into a unique hatchback ahead of its time – so that he could carry his drums in the back. It also was fitted with a Webasto fabric sunroof, cigar lighter, electric windows and reclining seats. Much later it was bought by Spice Girl singer 'Ginger Spice' Geri Halliwell.

Three of the classic Minis, George's, Paul's and Ringo's were re-united for a car show in London in 2023. Organisers claimed it was the first time they had been seen together since the recording of the White Album in 1968.

190 Le Indy 500
Very French car-maker Peugeot has won the all-American race, the Indy 500, three times – in 1913, 1916 and 1919.

191 Mad Mach
To try to change the image of electric cars in the US, Ford engineers built an extravagant high-powered version of its new Mach-E crossover.
The Mach-E 1400 is a fairly insane one-off model of Ford's electric crossover, the Mustang Mach-E. It is fitted with seven electric motors, three driving the front wheels, four driving the back. An extreme racing aerodynamic body kit is said to deliver a massive 2,300lbs of downforce at 160mph.

• As an extra promotional showdown Ford then pitched the Mach-E1400 against a sister creation the Mustang Cobra Jet 1400.
This is a 170mph rear-wheel drive super-sprint-race version of its all-electric crossover.
The two lined up side-by-side on a drag strip. The Mach-E pulled away from the line first, thanks to its four-wheel-drive traction. Once the rear-wheel-drive Cobra Jet got a grip on the tarmac however, it rocketed ahead of the bulkier Mach-E to win easily. The Cobra Jet reached 159mph (255kph) compared to the Mach-E's 135mph (217kph).

192 Worst country

A survey by the international Drivers Association compared road deaths, road quality, traffic and fuel prices across all the countries in Europe. It found the worst country to drive in on the continent is Romania, followed by Bulgaria and Bosnia.

193 Common faults

The five most common motoring offences and convictions in the UK are:

1 Speeding
2 Using phone at wheel
3 Ignoring traffic signal (like a red light)
4 Illegal/unauthorised parking
5 Moving offence, like driving wrong way down one-way street

194 A Prince's hearse

The former Duke of Edinburgh, the late Prince Philip, was passionate about Land Rovers.
On the day of his funeral in 2021, the prince's coffin was transported by a bronze-green Land Rover Td5 Defender 130. This military-inspired hearse was designed and adjusted by the Prince himself over the course of 16 years leading up to his death.
The British car brand also provided the family with three cars for the funeral.

195 Dirty driver

A fussy driving examiner failed a teenage learner – because there were some bits of rubber under the passenger seat. The car didn't even belong to the learner.

The family of the distraught test driver appealed over the result of the 2022 driving test in Lancashire, England. They explained that the test was conducted in their daughter's instructor's car. But driving test officials rejected the appeal. They said the car did not mean 'post-Covid cleanliness standards'.

The driving instructor had previously rubbed something out of his diary before the test and there were some tiny bits of his rubber left under the passenger seat. Other than that the car "was spotless" they complained.

Officials said their priority was "protecting public safety."

196 Luxury boom

In 2023 luxury car maker Bentley reported selling more than 15,000 vehicles globally, the highest sales figures since the company was formed in 1919.

197 Passing hotspots

An insurance company with too much time on its hands surveyed pass and fail rates of MOT tests in all the different areas of the UK.

The place where your vehicle is least likely to pass an MOT test is Kirkcaldy, Scotland, followed by Dundee, Scotland, and Truro, England.

In Kirkcaldy you are 14% more likely to fail your MOT test than in the area with the highest pass rate: Enfield in London.

198 Corolla joy

Multi-millionaire basketball star Jared Jeffries fulfilled a lifetime ambition by appearing on the TV game show The Price is Right – and won a car.

The 6ft 11in former New York Knicks forward won a Toyota Corolla worth just $22,000 (£18,000). The excited superstar joyously ran round the studio in celebration.

199 Anti clockwise

A used car dealer from North London was given a two-year suspended prison sentence in 2023 after police found he had sold 46 cars with 'clocked' mileages. Some of these had their milometer reading reduced by almost 80,000 miles.

Third gear
From the Notorious roller…
to the eternal dilemma

200 Cage fighting Rolls
Notorious MMA fighter Conor McGregor celebrated knocking
out opponent Jose Aldo in 13 seconds during a 2015 bout – by
rushing out and buying a £305,000 white Rolls Royce
Phantom Coupe.
The next year the luxury car brand saw an unusual
promotional opportunity to update its stuffy traditional image –
by gifting McGregor another car, this time a £280,000 Ghost
for free.
It was one of the least likely Rolls promotional vehicles ever –
a matt black luxury limousine with a huge graphic of
McGregor's face and tattoed torso along the side along with
his nickname 'NOTORIOUS' in large capitals.

201 Super Subaru
A blue and yellow WRC Subaru Impreza works rally car driven
by Richard Burns was a disaster during the 1999/2000 season
– it had to be retired twice due to serious transmission and
ignition issues. Despite this Burns went on to become world
champion the following year, this time in a different Subaru
Impreza.
But that original flopped blue and yellow car was bought by a
French enthusiast. He subjected it to a five-year, money-no-
object restoration. Finally it sold at auction in 2023 for
£520,000 ($650,000).

202 Parking block
Residents of a three-storey block of flats bizarrely built right in
the middle of a small roundabout in Aberdare, Wales, have
complained they have nowhere to park their cars.

203 Best brands
The two most profitable car companies in the world on the basis of return per car are Ferrari and Rolls Royce. Industry experts estimate the company owners, Fiat/Chrysler and BMW respectively, make around 50% return on their investment in the companies.

204 Royal Jeep
A humble World War Two jeep used by English King George VI for a morale-boosting visit to an American Flying Fortress bomber base during the conflict was recently sold at auction for £45,000.

205 Luxury spares
The world's largest independent stock of Rolls Royce and Bentley spares is held by Flying Spares, probably the world's most up-market scrapyard in Leicestershire, England. Its warehouse holds more than 180,000 bits of old Rolls and Bentleys.

Prices of parts include:
Rolls Royce official tax disk holder £10.79 ($13.21)
Windscreen wiper control knob (1955 Silver Wraith) £59.40 ($72.73)
Oil filter (1977 Corniche) £29.03 ($35.55)
Handbook (1939 Phantom) £123.74 ($151.52)
Recycled alloy wheel (2010 Cullinan) £1,440 ($1,763.34)
Reconditioned engine (1979 Silver Spirit) £14,394 ($17,626.03)

206 Equine fine
In Queensland, Australia it is illegal not to give way to a horse. Drivers must move to the side of the road, turn off their engine and wait if a horse rider signals that their horse is being hard to control. The rider can signal this by raising a hand and pointing at the horse. Drivers who fail to follow the rule can be hit with an Aus$130 fine (£74/US$90).

207 Disaster prize

A British family won a treasure hunt at a luxury holiday resort in Cyprus – but the prize almost killed them all.

The Tumbridge family were celebrating a 60th birthday at the resort and won a thrilling free Land Rover excursion through nearby mountains. However in a sudden rainstorm, their off-road excursion driver lost control and plunged from the dirt trail, over a cliff edge and down the mountain. The vehicle somersaulted twice and was stopped from falling hundreds of feet by crashing into a tree.

The family suffered minor injuries and are suing the holiday company. It was almost a "first prize to death" they complained.

208 Side steps

The Mercedes SLS AMG luxury supercar came with seats that could be adjusted in all the usual directions plus being able to move from side to side too.

209 Wonderful Wolseley

The biggest-selling car brand in Britain in the 1920s was Wolseley. The marque had been founded at the turn of the century by machine-gun manufacturers Hiram Maxim and the Vickers Brothers (Tom and Albert).

The name Wolseley came from a project to build a sheep-shearing machine run by the young engineer they appointed as their first managing director, Herbert Austin.

Five years later Austin left Wolseley to found his own car company. Austin went on to make Britain's best selling car of the thirties, the Austin Seven.

210 Sturdy supercar
Supercars are temperamental, fragile and difficult to own, right? Not for Arizona ceramic artist and motorist Sean Dirks, who bought a Honda/Acura NSX in 2004 and still has it.
The bright-red mid-engined Ferrari-beater is his everyday car and now has more than 400,000 miles on the clock. He has dealt with only two issues in that time, a replacement for worn-out suspension and a manual gearbox repair. The engine and electrics are original.

211 Shock tactics
Nine percent of car owners would like to be able to put an electric shock device on their car to stop anyone stealing it.

212 Dawn surprise
A brand new £350,000 Rolls Royce Dawn was stolen from its new owner's driveway in London, England – then discovered shortly afterwards in pieces in a shipping container bound for Dubai. Police believe the car was stolen to order.
The container was found at Thurrock Docks and also contained the dismantled parts of eight stolen Range Rovers.

213 Seaside stupidity
A driver was recently banned for a year in Adelaide, Australia – after she was convicted of speeding along a sandy beach, weaving between swim-suited sunbathers and toddlers building sandcastles. Amazingly no-one was hurt and her red Mazda S ended up bogged down in soft sand, enabling police to arrest the woman driver and impound the vehicle.

214 Low-slung Lancia

The Lancia Stratos HF was the first car specially designed for rallying.

The first Stratos was built by Nuccio Bertone who used the underpinnings of a friend's Lancia Fulvia and created the most eye-catching body shape round it, hoping to win a rally contract from Lancia.

He drove it to the gates of the Lancia factory where the car was so low slung it passed underneath the security barrier. The Lancia workers all burst into great applause and the management agreed to let him design their new rally car. His mid-engined oddity won the World Rally Championship three years running, in 1974, 1975 and 1976.

215 Optional oddities

Unusual optional extras offered by General Motors between 1950 – 1970:
(Thank you to Hemmings Auction house for intel on many of this lot)

• The 'Sportable' transistor radio (1958) could be slid out from its slot in the dashboard and taken anywhere to be listen to, running on its own batteries and aerial. When it was returned to the dashboard it would be powered by the car's own electrical system and play through the car's speakers.

• Throughout much of the fifties, GM offered Remington shavers as optional extras. They plugged into the car cigarette lighter via an adapter. It was considered an ideal feature for travelling salesmen. The shaver could be removed and plugged into the wall for home and hotel use.

•The 1967 Tempest, LeMans and GTO convertibles featured this extra: a vinyl tonneau cover to protect the open cockpit interior from sun, sand and dust. It came with a zipped section where the driver sits. So the owner could drive along with the top down and his body poking out above the tonneau that covered the rest of the car.

• Pontiacs came with an eight-track tape player mounted on the transmission tunnel behind the dashboard console so it was virtually impossible to operate while driving.

• From 1969 GM offered the Instant-Aire Pump extra. This cleverly inflated tyres up to 32psi using vacuum pressure from a port on the engine. Ironically it wasn't available on the 'Ram Air' models.

• In 1970 Pontiac offered the 'Rear Lamp Monitor'. This indicated to the driver in the rear view mirror whether the rear lights were working or not. The device was a small box on the rear parcel shelf connected to the rear lights via fibre optic cable, which illuminated when the lights did.

• Ventura hatchback owners had the chance to opt for a nylon tent device which fitted to the tailgate and normally stayed folded into its holder. When needed however it could extend the raised tailgate into an awning that formed a big enough space for two to sleep.

• In the early seventies GM suddenly became very litter conscious. Four different optional litter bins were offered to new car buyers. They fitted under the front or back seats in various ways. One even included a tissue dispenser.

• Seventies Pontiac buyers could opt for a CB short wave radio base station, not for the car, but for the home. The unit sported GM logos and featured traditional telephone-style handsets, loudspeakers and the ability to broadcast as a public address system.

• Some fifties models had a button on the floor to change the radio station with your foot while driving.

• Some early sixties Pontiacs came with an automatic cigarette dispenser. The driver could push a button under the dashboard and a few seconds later a cigarette would fall into a tray.

• Mid-fifties high-end GM convertible cars had a rain-sensor on the centre console. If it detected rain while parked, the sensor automatically raised the roof and closed the windows.

• In the mid sixties Buick cars featured a hook on the dashboard for female passengers to hang their handbags.

• The fifties Smoke-Out ashtray was an elaborate solution to cigarette smoke. It was powered by engine vacuum which sucked a cigarette butt from the ashtray into a sealed glass container in the engine bay.

• The seventies GM Tornado featured an exterior device with a circular rolling indicator to report the current outside temperature. It was mounted in a chrome housing on the driver's door, just ahead of the door mirror.

• The 1958 Pontiac Star Chief had a removable trunk light that extended on a power cable from a hidden reel for 15 feet. It could be used to illuminate changing any of the wheels after dark.

• Late sixties Camaros could come with 'Liquid Tire Chain' – a spray canister that squirted a special liquid all over the rear tyres. This supposedly aided winter driving by melting ice and snow.

• Some late-forties Chevy convertibles featured a tube low down under the door on the passenger side. Inside this was a special umbrella featuring the Chevy bowtie logo.

• Some 1968 LeMans came with a reverb unit for the radio. This added echo to the sound, a fashionable style at the time. One owner reported that 'the suspension was shot so every time the car bottomed out and the reverb was on, it would sound like a huge gong inside the car."

216 Banned after 49 minutes
In 2018 a German 18-year-old was banned from driving after being caught speeding at almost double the limit… just 49 minutes after passing his driving test.

217 TikTok triumph
Wolverhampton driving instructor Pin Binning has gathered 80 million likes and 1.4 million followers on Tik Tok – by posing difficult questions about Britain's Highway Code driving rules. The instructor, from England's West Midlands region, runs a driving school and trains other instructors.

218 Street race star

A legendary illegal Detroit street-racing muscle car from the seventies is due to be auctioned for millions of dollars in America at the time of writing.

Reading like a story from a movie, the Dodge Challenger has been revealed by descendants of its original owner. The car was locally famous as the 'Black Ghost'. It turned out to have been the secret hot-rod owned and driven by an off-duty Motor City cop who had awards for bravery.

The all-black supercharged car usually won its races on major routes like Woodward Avenue – then drove quickly from the scene to avoid detection.

219 Chinese Austin

The historic British car-making brand Austin, makers of the Austin Seven and Austin Mini, is now owned by China's largest state-owned motor manufacturer SAIC Motor Corp.

220 Rude racer

French motor racing star Alain Prost was World Champion four times and won a total of 51 F1 races – but he was also sacked twice from race teams for being rude about his car.

In 1983, despite finishing second in the driver's championship, he told TV reporters that his Renault RE40 was "not competitive" and that in his last race he "didn't lose by my own fault". He was fired two days later.

Then in 1991 he was fired by Ferrari F1 team for publicly moaning about the Ferrari 643, despite gaining six podium finishes in ten races. Proust told journalists that "a truck would be easier to drive than this car."

221 Petrol plus diesel
Lamborghini began as a tractor manufacturer in 1948. It devised a unique technological innovation for its Carioca tractors.

The fuel atomiser system allowed the tractors to be easily started with petrol – then switch to diesel for more fuel-efficient operation.

Soon Lamborghini was selling 200 Carioca tractors a year and by the early sixties was successful enough to start building supercars to challenge Ferrari*.

* Ferruccio Lamborghini had argued with Enzo Ferrari when he suggested improvements could be made to the Ferrari 250GT. The notoriously proud Ferrari dismissed him as a 'tractor-maker' so Lamborghini determined to retaliate. His first sports car was named 350GTV and he went on to create one of the world's most glamorous supercar brands.

222 Sign of extravagence
At a specialist auction in American in 2020 a car enthusiast paid for $40,120 (£33,300) for a 14ft/4.3m-tall yellow porcelain-and-neon sign from a Ford used-car lot in Oregon.

223 Rubber track
Australian researchers have found that adding rubber from old tyres to tarmac or asphalt makes road surfaces last twice as long before cracking. The ground tyre pieces make the road material twice as resistant to the effects of sunlight.

• Ford engineers are working with Rice University in Houston, Texas, to find a sophisticated new way to recycle vehicle plastics. Ford supplied plastic from old F-150 pickup trucks, including bumpers, gaskets and door panels. The university ground the plastics into powder, then zapped it with electricity to create graphene. This is returned to Ford where it is used as high-spec noise insulation in new vehicles.

• As a further twist, Ford sent some of the new noise insulation back to Rice who in turn were able to recycle it back to graphene again.

224 First lady of Fiat

Susanna Agnelli, the grand-daughter of Fiat founder Giovanni Agnelli and sister of Fiat boss Gianni Agnelli, was a successful politician who was the first female Foreign Minister of Italy. To those who claimed her career had been helped by her family's wealth, she pointed out that it had never been expected that she should have had a career at all. It was always assumed that the "boys", not Susanna, would run the Fiat empire.

225 Swimming car

The Volkswagen Type 166 was known as the Schwimmwagen – a four-wheel drive amphibious military vehicle used extensively by the Germans in the Second World War. The Beetle-based 'swim wagen' is the most-produced amphibious vehicle ever, with more than 15,000 being built. It had a propeller that was lowered into position when in the water and powered it at 6mph. Unfortunately it could only operate in a forward direction. Rudimentary steering was achieved by turning the wheels – or by the passengers using paddles.

226 Stunt double

Stuntman Bud Ekins performed two of the most famous movie stunts of all time when he was Steve McQueen's stunt double. Ekins was actually born and lived in Hollywood, learning his skills riding and driving off-road in the Hollywood Hills. Firstly in The Great Escape (1963), Ekins escaped the prison by jumping the prison fence on a motorbike. Then he was also the driver in one of the best-known car chases in film history. He was at the wheel of a Ford Mustang 390 GT through the streets of San Francisco in the 1968 film Bullitt.

227 Stretch or shrink

The wheelbase of a car is the distance between the centre of its axles.

Many cars are available with a longer wheelbase version – to increase the space and sense of luxury. These include: Mercedes S Class, Rolls Royce Phantom and Jeep Wrangler. Other cars are produced with a short wheelbase, to add to the sport looks and handling of a longer saloon version. These include the Honda Accord Coupe, Ferrari 250 and Audi Quattro.

228 Bright & breezy

The word 'breezeway' is used by car designers to describe models fitted with a rear window that was retractable. These were mostly fifties and sixties Mercurys.

The rear window was slightly convex slanted and was lowered into the trunk at the press of a button. It created a much greater through-ventilation than opening the side windows as is more normal, hence the name 'breezeway'.

229 Fatal tube

The experimental Dymaxion car was unveiled at the 1933 Chicago World Fair. It was a strange tubular three-wheeler with a periscope.

The Dymaxion was created by eccentric inventor Bucky Fuller and named after his principles of 'Dynamic Maximum Tension'. It had a rear V8 engine driving the front wheels, an aluminium body on an ash wood frame and was steered by its single rear wheel.

On a break from appearing at the World Fair, the Dymaxion went on a drive along Lake Shore Drive. The car tried to make a sharp turn but skidded, rolled over four times and was hit by another vehicle driven by a shoe salesman.

Fuller's test driver Frank Turner was killed and two passengers badly injured.

230 Minor success

The first British passenger vehicle to sell over a million cars was the Morris Minor.

The curvy family car was produced from 1948 until 1972. During its lifespan there were two-door saloons, convertibles, four-door saloons, wooden framed tourers (called the Traveller), panel vans and pick-up versions.

It was designed by Sir Alec Issigonis, who later created the Mini. More than 1.6 million Minors were eventually built. Today it is often picked as a car that defines a traditional 'Englishness'.

231 Best of the best

In 2022 the specialist website Engineering.com picked its best cars of all time. It chose the Citroen DS – "the first mass production car to feature hydropneumatic suspension and disc brakes. The body was aerodynamic decades before this became standard for production cars, with features such as adjustable ride height and self-levelling that are still not common in production cars today."

Meanwhile in 2021 Autoexpress magazine chose the best-looking cars of all time. The 'top ten most beautiful cars' was decided as:

10 Corvette Stingray 1963
9 Ford GT40 1964
8 Lamborghini Countach 1974
7 Aston Martin Valkyrie 2021
6 Hispano H6B Tulipwood 1924
5 Mercedes 540K Spezial Roadster 1936
4 Bugatti Type 57 Atlantic 1935
3 Jaguar XK120 1954
2 Ferrari 250 GT California Spyder SWB 1960
1 Alfa 8C 2900 Mille Miglia 1938

232 Prancing producer
Everyone knows Ferrari builds its own engines for its Formula One cars. It is less well known that it has also built the engines for many other teams, including Haas (2023), Alfa Romeo (2023), Marussia (2014), Force India (2008), Suderia Toro Rosso (2007-16), Spyker (2007), Red Bull (2006), Prost (2001), Sauber (1997-2005) and Minardi (1991).

233 Part peril
A British woman was horrified to find her car was stripped for parts while she was at a concert at the O2 Academy in Birmingham in 2022. Her Citroen C1 was just a shell when she returned to the car park.

* A charity worker in Birmingham had the front bumper stolen from her Ford Fiesta while it was parked in the city centre. She bought a replacement bumper but within two months this too was stolen while it was parked. "The person I bought the bumper from is probably the one who stole it," she lamented.

234 Drag power
A nitro-methane powered top fuel dragster with a 500 cubic inch V8 engine can produce around 12,000bhp – that's twelve times as much power as an F1 racing car. Each of the drag car's cylinders produces around 1,500bhp.

235 Genital clanger
Promotional social media by VW's Italian operation went globally viral for all the wrong reasons after the company's Italia Instagram account was unfortunately titled volkswagenitalia.

236 Core offence
British drivers could be given an on-the-spot fine of up to £150 if caught throwing an old apple core out of the window. Throwing something outside can be classed as littering - even if the item is biodegradable or an animal immediately comes along and eats it.

237 Big Mac whack

Bob Spink from Bath, England, suffered one of the world's most expensive drive-through meals.

After buying a burger at a MacDonald's drive-through he found that the car park was full. So the 50-year-old stopped to eat it in the Starbuck's car park next door.

His 16-minute stay in the rival company parking space however was automatically monitored and he was registered as a 'non-patron'. A few days later he received a penalty charge of £100 from Starbuck's through the post.

238 Ammonia motor

US engineering firm Amogy unveiled the world's first ammonia-powered tractor in 2022. The large John Deere farm machine is able to plough fields and drive across farmland as normal – while creating zero emissions say the makers.

Amogy are also planning to build large trucks and cargo ships powered by the unfamiliar chemical.

239 VW bangers

Volkswagen sells more sausages than cars. The German manufacturer sells more than 7 million 'currywurst' VW-branded sausages a year.

240 Motor City drive-by

The Motor Cities National Heritage Area is a specially designated part of southern Michigan where much of America's automobile industry was created and operated.

The region around Detroit includes more than 1,200 motoring-related sites ranging from major sights like the Automotive Hall of Fame, Henry Ford Museum, Fair Lane (Ford's home) and Sloan Museum to lesser known ones like the Cadillac Museum, Horace Dodge's home and longstanding Chick Inn Drive-In.

Today tourists are offered guided tours of the area in a Ford Model-A.

241 Car pool

In a bizarre cartoon-like sequence, a Tesla driver accidentally pressed the accelerator instead of the brake, causing their car to speed right through a brick wall into a suburban garden – where it plunged into a family swimming pool.

Three passengers were rescued as the car sank.

The white luxury EV was later photographed by fire department staff still floating in the pool of the Spanish-style villa in Pasadena, New Mexico, USA – which happened to be owned by a top Disney executive.

242 Dames' Dodge

In the mid-fifties car-makers became aware of the growing market for women buying their own cars.

In 1955 Dodge introduced the La Femme, based on their Custom Royal model. It came with colour options 'Heather Rose', 'Misty Orchid' and 'Regal Orchid'. On-board accessories included a raincoat, umbrella and a tube of lipstick.

Dodge's advertising team titled their brochure for the car: "By Appointment to Her Majesty, the American Woman."

243 Banned plates

UK authorities ban car number plates that are deemed rude or offensive. The latest batch to be banned by the DVLA include:
Any containing the three letters ARS, DAM, DCK, SEX, BUM, ASS or WNK.
Any containing five-digit combinations like this:
B**UMS, FA**RTY and CR**PS.
Other recent one-off bans by the British registration authorities include:
BE22 END
BU22 SHT
CO22 ONA
DR22 NK
F22 KER
GB22 BAD
M22 FKR
PU22 SSY
RA22 APE
S22 LAG
TE22 ROR
TU22 URD
UK22 GUN
UP22 BOM
WE22 GAY
YE22 DTH
YS22 WAR

244 Faulty tech

A study of reliability of cars by British consumer journalists found that 31% of electric cars were suffering issues requiring garage attention compared to 19% of petrol ones. Just to complicate matters hybrid cars were the most reliable, with only 17% developing a fault per year.

245 Banger accident

A British driver's nose was broken by a frozen sausage that was thrown through the window of his car. An Essex ambulance spokesman said: "He was making his way home after work with the window down because it was such a nice afternoon. He saw a car coming the other way and felt a searing pain in his nose. Luckily he managed to stop his car without hitting anyone else."

246 Policy limits

An un-named woman from Missouri, USA, made a claim for $5.2 million/£4.3m against a man's car insurance policy – because she said he was liable after she caught a sexually-transmitted disease after conducting a relationship in his vehicle.

The award was initially approved by courts but eventually the state Supreme Court overturned the ruling in 2023. The insurance company defended the claim saying the injury did not occur during 'normal use of the vehicle'.

247 Miracle Merc

Mercedes engineers took an independent observer for a drive to demonstrate their new Vision EQXX eco-car in 2022. The electric car uses solar panels and downhill recharging systems to top up its batteries.

The ultra-light, low-drag 241bhp coupe drove from Stuttgart in Germany, over the Alps into Italy and west into the French Riviera. The drive ended after 12 hours on a beach near Marseilles.

Average speed was 87kph/54mph with top speeds of 140kph/87mph. In total, the Vision concept car had covered 1008km (626 miles) without a single stop to recharge. The company claims that the 'most efficient Mercedes ever built' still had 15 per cent of its battery charge remaining at the end.

248 Mystery puddles

In 2023 a leading British breakdown service published this list of seven signs that your car needs a service:

1 A light saying 'SERVICE' illuminates on the dashboard

2 Strange noises
Clicks, hisses, ticks, and squeaking could all indicate a problem under the bonnet. If the sound is becoming more intense or the problem seems urgent, you should pull over as soon as it's safe to do so and call a mechanic right away.

3 Mystery Puddles
Your car can leak water through condensation in the air-con unit in the summer, or your exhaust in the winter. Either way, both scenarios are harmless and won't need the attention of a mechanic.
If your car leaks coloured liquid, you could have a more serious problem on your hands.
Brown liquid could be a sign that you're leaking power steering fluid, oil, or the most serious of them all, brake fluid. If you suspect you're missing vital fluid, you shouldn't attempt to drive your car at all, not even for a service.

4 Power loss
There could be a number of reasons for the problems in your car and sometimes there's a very simple fix. Spark plugs could be faulty and thankfully replacing them is a straightforward and inexpensive job, but it's best to leave it to the professionals. Alternatively, your fuel injection system could be malfunctioning and starving your engine of fuel or oxygen. A clogged catalytic converter could also be disrupting airflow, a simple service will help to diagnose the problem.

5 Brakes behaving differently
A mechanic will be able to pinpoint the problem during a service and replacing brake pads is usually a simple process. Remember, it's best to call a professional out to your car for repairs rather than risk your brakes failing as you drive to an RAC-approved garage.

6 Smoke from the bonnet or exhaust
If the smoke appears to come from a fire under your bonnet, you should turn off your engine.

7 Vibrations
If you've noticed unusual movements in your car, there could be a number of potential explanations. For example, juddering while pulling away could be due to worn-out friction material or a pressure plate defect – perhaps a combination of both. It could also be caused by an oil leak contaminating the clutch plate.
If your car judders or vibrates at low revs, the engine mount which holds the engine in place could be loose, worn or broken.

249 Least safe
The latest official verdicts from the Euro NCAP testing organisation judge that the LEAST safe new vehicles on Europe's roads are the Renault Zoe and Dacia Spring.

250 Pothole peak
The worst month for potholes causing damage to British cars is March. This one month has double the number of claims for pothole damage compared to September, according to a survey by a UK motor insurance company that really should find something better to do with its time.

251 Hot hut
Eccentric British charity fundraiser Kevin Nicks built a wooden shed capable of over 100mph. Kevin's vehicle was made of shiplap wood panels and an apex felted roof bolted to VW Passat underpinnings. The whole thing is powered by an Audi twin-turbo V6.
When tested on the famous Pendine Sands speed strip the shed hit 101mph, enabling Kevin to claim it is the world's fastest shed.

252 Drink ban
Drivers in the sun-baked Mediterranean island of Cyprus are legally forbidden from drinking water while at the wheel.

253 Smart scarf
Mercedes have combined a new engineering technology with a traditional idea to come up with the 'Airscarf' feature in their premium open-top vehicles. This heating system uses vent in the seat back, just below the headrest, to mimic wearing a warm scarf. It blows hot air on the back of your neck when the car's roof is down on a cooler day.

254 Affordable Olds
The first vehicle to be marketed as an 'economy car' was the Oldsmobile Curved Dash or Model R. The two-seater open car was the first passenger vehicle built on a production line using interchangeable parts.
More than 19,000 were built between 1901 and 1907. Cars were still considered luxury purchases but the 20mph (32kph) Oldsmobile launched with a price tag of US$650, the equivalent of around $20,000 now.

255 Drink crash
A driver celebrated the end of an enforced sober spell by drinking so much he crashed into three cars parked outside a Conservative Party social club.
He was spotted on CCTV clambering from his car, then reaching back inside to retrieve his cans of Stella Artois lager. The motorist in Torquay, England, had just reached the end of a three-month alcohol abstinence order imposed for a previous offence. He was soon caught by police and given a 10-month suspended jail sentence and sent for mandatory alcohol treatment.

266 Inventor's triumph

American inventor Robert Kearns invented the intermittent windscreen wiper in 1963. He pitched his invention to America's big three car manufacturers who rejected it and promptly produced their own versions of his idea.

Kearns wasn't prepared to bow to the might of the global corporations however. He single-handedly took Ford, Chrysler and GM to court for stealing his idea.

Eventually, after 30 years of legal battling he won recognition that he invented the intermittent system – and received more than $30 million in damages.

267 Made in Canada

The Oshawa Car Assembly Plant in Ontario, Canada is one of the world's biggest car factories. It began as a site building cars for Chevrolet in 1907 and has made millions of cars including 1920s Cadillacs, 1960s Buick Skylarks and Chevrolet Impalas (200-2019). At the time of writing it makes GM's Silverado pick-up trucks.

268 Wooden extras

Overfinch's Holland & Holland special Range Rover edition relies on handcrafted features rather than the latest technology. This involves fitting a hand-made wood veneer drinks cabinet and boot-mounted shotgun case complete with engraved metal inlays of gunmaker Holland & Holland's diamond-shaped logo throughout.

269 Gadget watch

Aston Martin joined forces with high-end fashion brand Jaeger-LeCoultreto create the DBS Transponder Watch, which costs around £12,500/$16,330. It's a very stylish and functional watch but it also has a suitably James Bond-ish feature too – the ability to open and close the doors of your Aston Martin simply by pressing the glass face.

270 UK motoring survey

Another British motor insurance company spent its profits doing a survey in 2023, which it then sent to motoring writers like me who usually put it straight in the bin. Except I've got a book o fill, so I'll report this one briefly for you:

Preston is the British city with the best drivers. That's if you number-crunch all the figures for fatal, serious and slight traffic accidents and combine them with driving test pass rates and first-time pass rates.

Yes, it's nonsense but if you're interested, the full line-up is:
1. Preston, 2. Aberdeen, 3. Cardiff, 4. Norwich, 5. Chichester, 6. Dundee, 7. London, 8. Newport, 9. Chelmsford, 10. Southend-on-Sea.

271 Driving test fail

A woman taking her driving test in Argentina in 2023 lost control and rolled her car – even though she was driving slowly round a junction on a special replica road layout at the driving test centre. CCTV footage of the incident became viral as it showed her mounting a kerb then mysteriously accelerating, careering into a lamppost and completely overturning.

271 A Prince's first car

Prince William, the Duke of Cambridge, started his driving career in a Ford Focus. The Prince passed his practical test at the age of 17 after taking about 20 driving lessons.

For his 17th birthday, William received a Volkswagen Golf from his father, now King Charles.

Coincidentally, Kate Middleton, his future wife and Duchess of Cambridge, owned a VW Golf around the same time too. She bought it before driving off to university.

272 Sewn together
Charles Singer of the sewing machine company and wealthy entrepreneur Henry Palmer combined forces in 1911 to create 'The Best in Motor Cars': the Palmer-Singer.

The 4-50 seven-seater was a grand convertible of the brass era. Four were built. At the latest count, three survive more than 110 years later. One sold recently at auction for around half a million US dollars.

273 Slow and happy
A dedicated fan of the 2021 car movie Fast and Furious tried to dodge copyright laws by uploading the entire film one Tweet at a time.

The fan eventually posted 52 different Tweets, each showing two-minute sections of the film. The (X) Twitter account was later suspended.

274 Speed limit
British speed cameras only click into action if a motorist passes at 10% over the limit plus 2mph. So drivers can theoretically get away with driving at 24mph in a 20mph limit or 35mph in a 30mph zone.

275 Baby snatch
Car thieves jumped into an open Volkswagen SUV that had stopped for a moment outside a shop. They drove off while the owner was unaware in the shop – but screeched to a halt after just 350 metres. They found that a two-year-old toddler was asleep in the back seat.

The panicking robbers lifted the boy from his car seat and simply left him on the pavement – then drove off again. The boy was found unharmed and the two thieves were soon caught, arrested and charged with a string of offences by police in Melbourne, Australia.

276 Pioneer prang

The first recorded car crash in America was in Ohio City in 1891. A pioneering automobile inventor called James William Lambert was testing his single-cylinder horseless carriage in Ohio City. He hit a tree root in the road and swerved into a wooden post. He and his passenger, James Swoveland a local drugstore owner, sustained minor injuries.

277 Super SUV

At the end of 2022 US manufacturer Drako launched an extraordinary new luxury SUV. The five-seater Dragon four-wheel-drive off-roader has an electric motor so powerful it can accelerate the large vehicle from 0-60mph in just 1.9 seconds. The Californian-built Dragon costs US$290,000.

278 Swiss role

Researchers studied fuel prices, road quality, traffic congestion and accident statistics to discover which is the most 'car-friendly' country in Europe. The answer was: Switzerland. The mountainous country has lots of well-made and maintained roads through spectacular landscapes, very low accident rates and few traffic jams.
Second best is the Netherlands, third is Belgium. The UK is the 18th most car-friendly, behind Iceland, Turkey and Hungary.

279 Dirty Olds man

When Oldsmobile decided to send its pioneering new car to the New York Automobile Show of 1901 it wasn't quite as easy as delivering a new car might be today. Olds sent professional test driver Roy Chapin (who later founded the Hudson Motor Company and then served as US Secretary of Commerce) to drive the car direct from the Michigan factory all the way to NYC.

It took eight days, including a long and muddy stretch along the Erie Canal Towpath.

When Chapin arrived to claim his room at the Waldorf Astoria Hotel he was so mud-splattered he was turned away at the door. In the end he was able to gain entry via the rear servants' entrance.

Luckily the new Oldsmobile Curved Dash model was cleaned up for the show and went on to sell hundreds of cars to visiting dealers.

280 Funny Ford

Carlos and Gladys Sierra from Weston-Super-Mare in the UK like their Ford Sierra estate, despite the jokes they get.

"People call me 'Ford' for a laugh, but I don't mind," says the council carpenter. "It was worse when I had a Cortina estate and everyone kept saying 'you ought to get a Sierra'. I was actually quite apprehensive when I went to buy it because of the mickey-taking but now we think it's a good car.

"A policeman came last week to investigate an attempted theft of petrol from the car and he was called PC Ford. We had a good laugh when I told him what my name was."

281 No cameras

The police force of the English county of Durham has fitted no fixed speed enforcement cameras anywhere on its road network. Not one.

The nearby county of West Yorkshire by contrast has 402 speed cameras on its roads.

282 Animal rules
On South African roads an animal always has the right of way. In the United Arab Emirates the law is that camels always have a right of way on any road.
In the US state of Tennessee drivers are not allowed to shoot an animal from their vehicle.

283 Royal wheels
The disgruntled second son of King Charles III, Prince Harry, nevertheless shares his family's passion for expensive cars. Famously after his wedding he was pictured whisking his new bride Meghan away in a Jaguar E-Type Concept Zero, an electric version of one of the brand's most iconic designs.
He's also been seen in the driving seat of a Jaguar F-Type, a two-seater luxury sports car.
Harry was also the owner of an Audi RS6 Avant, which he used to drive himself and Meghan to his sister-in-law Pippa Middleton's wedding reception. However, after clocking up just 4,500 miles, he sold this Audi in 2018 for £71,900.

284 Hole story
In a recent report about the state of Britain's road surfaces it was revealed that over a two-month period RAC patrols attended more than 1,400 breakdowns... that were caused by potholes.
Officials at the road surfacing trade body, the Asphalt Industry Alliance, promptly replied to the report. They claimed that they are working so hard to make road repairs that on average one pothole is being filled somewhere in the UK every 19 seconds.

285 Sheikh's collection

Sheikh Hamad bin al Nahyan has one of the world's weirdest car collections. The eccentric billionaire royal from the United Arab Emirates once paid to have a series of canals that spelled out his first name carved into an island located off the Abu Dhabi coast.

His car collection includes the world's largest SUV, an Oshkosh M1075 all-terrain ten-wheeler 15-litre army truck with a Jeep Wrangler cockpit stuck on top for him to sit in. It's 35ft long (10.8m) and 10 feet high (3.2m).

There's also a giant Land Rover that is too big to actually move but his mammoth Willys Jeep does. It's a 21ft-tall exact replica of a wartime Jeep and is driven from a seat hidden in the engine bay behind the front grille.

The Sheikh also has a Mercedes S-Class luxury saloon fitted with huge monster truck wheels, another that's been gold-plated and a third that has been fitted with gull-wing doors. His Citroen DS, Traction Avant, VW Beetle Dune Buggy and 1967 Honda N600 hardly seem worth mentioning in comparison.

286 Insurance fraud

An Uber Eats delivery driver from Oxfordshire, England, crashed into a country house, causing £85,000 worth of damage. While the car was still embedded in the side of the house, the driver was seen frantically speaking on his phone. Later it was revealed the 28-year-old Audi driver had been arranging a motor insurance policy to start that day. Insurance fraud investigators took a year to realise the connection between the date of the claim and the date of the policy starting.

The driver was taken to court where it was revealed that he had actually opened the policy 12 minutes AFTER the accident he had claimed for.

287 Drinking districts

The booziest drivers in Britain are in Cambridgeshire a recent survey has shown. Researchers looked at the percentage of breath tests that are positive across the UK.

The affluent Eastern county of Cambridgeshire topped the table – with 33.5% of tests of motorists there being positive. The nearest rival in the drink-drive records is Gloucestershire, with 27% positive tests.

The least boozy drivers meanwhile are found in the rural southwestern counties of Devon and Cornwall. Out of 10,687 breathalisers conducted in those two counties only 11% were positive. Lincolnshire and Hampshire were close behind with 11.4% and 11.7% respectively.

288 Woman driver

The first woman to gain a driving licence in America in 1900 was Anne Rainsford French Bush from Washington DC. She was only 21 and became a familiar sight in the Capitol Hill neighbourhood driving her steam-powered car. She was famous for always being seen driving with one hand on her hat to stop it flying off.

289 Room with a view

A British sportscar manufacturer has worked with an architect to construct a house in Japan. 'The Aston Martin House' is an expensive luxury modern home in an affluent Tokyo suburb. The house has a rooftop terrace, wine cellar, cinema, gym and spa – and includes a huge glass-fronted garage to display the owner's Aston Martins. The spacious dining room is designed so occupants and their visitors can gaze at the car collection through a glass wall while they are eating.

290 Parking fail hit

A Hong Kong motorist was shown on social media trying to back into a space in a multi-storey car park – for eight minutes. His dozens of hopeless attempts to get into the average-sized parking slot made for a rather dull film but it was an unlikely hit with millions of views.

291 Drink seizures

Latvia has one of Europe's highest drink-driving rates. In 2023 in order to aid the Ukranian war effort the Latvian government began seizing 100 cars a month from convicted drunk drivers and shipping them to Ukraine for use by hospitals and the military.

292 Hot car

In a race at Brooklands in 1937 dashing Old Etonian driver Tony Rolt took immediate innovative action to save the day when a bolt dropped off the exhaust of his ERA Remus open-top racing car.

It caused flames to flash into the cockpit and start swirling around his lap. While cornering at speed Rolt calmly took off one of his driving gloves and stuffed it in the hole in the exhaust.

The unique mechanical solution fixed the problem – and of course Rolt went on to win the race.

293 Star's cars

British upper-crust movie star Benedict Cumberbatch is an unlikely car collector. His garage at the last inspection includes a 1959 Chevrolet Bel Air, 2022 Audi E-Tron GT, Jaguar XJ (2019), Lamborghini Huracan (2019), Mercedes S Class (2021) and Lamborghini Urus (2019).

294 Global dominance

Until 1906 the French dominated global car production, building more of the new horseless carriages than the UK, Germany and the US. After 1907 American car-making finally took over as the biggest in the world.

- By 1927 America made 85% of the world's cars. In fact by 1920 the state of Michigan alone had more cars than the whole of the UK and Ireland. In 1923 even a sparsely populated state like Kansas had more cars than the whole of France or Germany.

295 Badge engineering

In 2013 Honda recalled all models of the Odyssey people carrier. The company decided it had sometimes stuck the 'Odyssey' badge on the wrong side of the tailgate. The badge should be on the driver's side but many were on the passenger side by mistake. Honda wanted to make sure they all matched – in case it affected resale value.

* In 1995 Toyota recalled 627,858 Corollas for an urgent repair at their nearest dealers. The company discovered a design fault: the drinks holder in the centre console was right next to the airbag trigger sensor. If drinks spilled they could activate the airbag suddenly.

296 Love driving

A male driver stopped by traffic police on Britain's M40 motorway was driving at 102mph on Easter Sunday 2022. He told them "love made me do it."
The driver told officers he was on his way to see his girlfriend. Thames Valley Police retorted that "love is not a valid reason for travelling at 42mph over the speed limit."

297 Road loads

Almost 90% of America's freight cargo is carried by road.

298 Guilty prints

British police easily caught a car thief who stole a Ford Fiesta during a snowstorm in Cheshire in January 2023. They found the car parked in Runcorn and simply followed footprints in the fresh show right to the thief's house nearby.

299 Driving questions

Buzzfeed listed these '13 Inexplicable questions we all have while driving':

1 Everyone came to the four-way stop at the same time. Who goes first?

2 There's a line of police cars behind me trying to get by. Speed up or slow down?

3 The same guy keeps pulling up next to me at every red light. Do I acknowledge him every time?

4 A hitchhiker looks upbeat and friendly. Will he rob me?

5 I've been driving automatics for years. Is that pedal the clutch or the accelerator? (you'll soon find out)

6 I've dropped my fries. Clean up now or later?

7 Ask for directions or curl up and die?

8 My engine light just came on. False alarm or serious problem?

9 A pedestrian just made a rude sign. Do it back or take the moral high ground?

10 I'm late. The only parking space is reserved. Should I pretend I didn't notice? (depends how much you like the look of your car)

11 We're not moving. Would the other lane be better?

12 We're all singing along and I just sang a different lyric to everyone else. Should I slowly stop singing?

13 That was the last rest stop for 20 miles. Can I wait that long?

Fourth gear
From the racing princes… to dodged tickets

300 Racing princes
Two Siamese princes, Chula Chakrabongse and Bira
Birabongse Bhanudej Bhanubandh became famous in
international motor racing before the second world war.
The duo were not only cousins, they were both Old Etonians.
They formed a team called White Mouse Racing based in
Hammersmith in London.
The main driver was known as Bira for short. He was a crown
prince of Siam, now called Thailand, where his grandfather
was the inspiration for the musical The King and I.
Bira was also a daredevil aristocrat in the style of the time. His
antics included driving a racing car in Formula One, being an
accomplished sports sailor, competing in four Olympics, and
being an aviator who once flew his own plane solo from
London to Bangkok. During World War II he taught flying to
RAF pilots at an airfield in Cornwall.
Prince Chula meanwhile was less of a driver but financed the
team – and wrote 13 books, mostly about motor racing.
At first Prince Bira drove a Riley Imp at Brooklands for the
team. It was painted in the style of a dress of a Scandinavian
woman Bira had met in London. This later evolved to become
the national racing colours of Siam, pale blue with yellow.
In 1935 Prince Chula bought Bira a powerful ERA racing car
nicknamed 'Romulus'. Bira finished second in his first race in
the ERA – despite having to stop to make emergency repairs
halfway through the race. The next season Bira won at Monte
Carlo and four other circuits.
The Bira race circuit just outside Pattaya, Thailand, is named
after the prince.

301 Helping Hans

Wealthy merchant banker Hans Van Hock bought a brand new Bentley S1 Sports Saloon in 1958 for his wife Johanna who was a member of the Institute of Advanced Motorists.

Hans, in contrast, was evidently a hopeless driver, according to his wife. Hans sometimes used the Bentley but believed he didn't need to signal when turning at junctions.

So his wife had a second indicator switch installed on the passenger side. She used this unique extra to indicate for him when he was making any manoeuvres while driving.

302 Are you sitting comfortably?

The most advanced car seat in the world, ever, is probably the REAR seat in a 2022 Bentley Bentayga.

Bentley's advanced 'airline-seat' system is an option chosen by around 50% of buyers. It automatically makes microscopic three-dimensional adjustments to the passenger's seating position throughout a journey. It particularly targets their pressure points where their legs and back touch the seat using an algorithm developed in collaboration with a chiropractor.

The Bentayga system uses 12 silent electric motors to offer 22 directions of adjustment and also use three intelligent pneumatic valves controlled by a central 'wellbeing and seat motion' ECU computer. The combination of these units can apply 177 individual pressure changes across six pressure zones on the passenger's body over a three-hour period. This is designed to improve comfort and minimise fatigue during long seated journeys.

Also by monitoring the temperature of different parts of the passenger to an accuracy of 0.1 degree C every 25 milliseconds the temperatures of the seat surface can be precisely controlled.

By subtly and imperceptibly changing the shape and warmth of the surfaces of the seat, no one area of the body endures fatigue for an extended period – to ensure the occupant always feels comfortable, say Bentley.

There are also adjustable leg and footrests, extra cushion and backrest adjustments and powered headrest adjustment.

The nearside passenger can be deemed important enough to deploy the car's 'VIP mode'. In this mode the REAR passenger can move the FRONT passenger seat forward to give themselves more leg room. That's fine if you are a chauffered billionaire or celebrity, less good if you're normal and the kids are in the back seat.

303 Holy outcome

American car-makers started making holes in their vehicles rear bumpers/fenders in the late 1950s. This was a styling trend to allow the exhaust to flow through.

The idea was that the long, low-slung cars of the time could foul their exhaust pipes on the ground if they protruded behind the car's extended rear overhang.

Instead two holes in the back of your fender was thought to be classy as it symbolised you had twin exhausts. This design was fitted to V8 cars like Cadillac, Lincoln, Imperial and Packard.

The fashion didn't last long however. Owners found that the rear underside of the car rotted rapidly if exhaust was allowed to billow underneath. The acidic content of the soot that caked the underneath of the car ate into the metal.

304 Winning wheels

Here are the seven best steering wheels of all time, according to motorsport venue Goodwood.com

1 Citroen DS – the futuristic plastic single-spoke wheel from 1955 featured a Citroen logo but no buttons or controls.

2 Lancia Stratos – an oddly macho wheel from the seventies with six exposed bolt heads, simple metal frame and small leather-covered rim.

3 Subaru XT – the quirky eighties coupe offered a black plastic wheel with asymmetrical L-shaped spokes and centre boss, which housed two buttons for the cruise control.

4 Ferrari 250GT – the late fifties wheel was an elegant thin-rimmed but large-diameter wooden wheel with three polished alloy spokes.

5 Chrysler 300J – the two-spoke squared-off oval wheel from 1963 featured a strange shinier inner wheel held by its own pair of metallic spokes within the outer wheel.

6 ItalDesign Maserati Boomerang Prototype – only a concept car from 1972 but, still, what a wheel! All the instruments are housed in a circular round binnacle like a big saucepan and the wheel rotates around the rim of this tub-shaped dashboard. The shape meant that drivers have to steer with their palms.
7 Lotus Elan – the original sixties Elan had a classy and simple wood wheel decorated with three drilled-alloy spokes.

305 Landmark demolished

Pioneering car engineer and businessman Roy Chapin commissioned acclaimed architect John Pope to build a grand colonnaded house for his family on prestigious Lake Shore Road in Michigan. A former car test driver, Chapin had founded the Hudson Motor Company and later served as US Secretary of Commerce.

The house was a noted landmark, set in landscaped grounds, which included an avenue of 600-year-old yews imported from England. After Chapin's death in 1936 his wife Inez continued to live in the house for another 20 years.

But when she died, rival motor manufacturer Henry Ford II bought the house – and deliberately demolished it. Ford then built apartment blocks on Chapin's former lakeside land.

306 Fast talking

The car's accelerator pedal is also called a gas pedal, throttle, loud pedal, hammer, gas and gun.

Pressing the accelerator pedal has even more synonyms, including: step on the gas, press go, put pedal to the metal, make tracks, burn rubber, step on it, open the throttle, nail it, and hit the gas.

307 Editor's expedition

The first editor of Britain's Autocar magazine, the oldest motoring publication in the world, was Henry Sturmey. After launching the magazine in 1895 Sturmey became the first motorist to ever drive the full length of Britain, from Land's End to John O'Groats. The 874-mile journey in a Daimler 4.5hp took ten days at an average speed of 10mph.

Today Google Maps tells motorists the journey will take 14 hours 40 minutes.

308 Video star

A TV reality show promised to take players of the Gran Turismo video race game and tutor them in real race-car driving. The GT Academy attracted 25,000 entrants across Europe.

The winner of the first series was young 24-year-old unknown Spaniard Lucas Ordonez, whose prize was a chance to drive in the 2009 Dubai 24 Hour race, sharing the car with Johnny Herbert. Ordonez turned out to be so good that Nissan offered him a driver's seat in a 350Z for the next season in the GT4 European Cup.

Ordonez was placed in his first race and finished the season second, with two wins and six podium finishes. He has since become a successful professional racing driver.

309 Highway jams

The latest traffic speed data has revealed America's most congested highways. They are:
1 I-94 Fort Lee, NJ
2 I-294/I-290 Chicago, IL
3 I-45/I-69 Houston, TX
4 I-285/I-85 Atlanta, GA
5 I-20/I-285 Atlanta, GA
6 I-290/I-90 Chicago, IL
7 SR60/SR57 Los Angeles, CA
8 I-710/I-105 Los Angeles, CA
9 I-24/I-40 Nashville, TN
10 1-10/1-15 San Bernardino, CA

310 Automatic farmer

What could be more polluting than a chugging old diesel farm tractor? That is the motivation for the innovative new Monarch MK-V electric tractor. Monarch claim that replacing an old diesel tractor is equivalent to replacing 14 internal combustion-engined cars.

The Californian-produced vehicle can run for 14-hours – with or without a human driver. A system of cameras and computers allows the tractor to work on the farm autonomously.

311 Heat peril
The NHTSA reported 33 children died of heatstroke after being left in American parked cars in 2022.

312 Uni-body tank
The first mass-produced uni-body car (where the body and frame are one welded unit) produced in America was the Nash 600, built by the Nash-Kelvinator Corporation of Wisconcin from 1941.
The 600 name signified the car's ability to travel 600 miles (970km) on one tank of fuel. The fuel economy was only around 30mpg so, in order to achieve that 600 distance, the car needed a big tank. It held 20 US gallons/76 litres.

313 Fiero brigade
The exciting mid-engined Pontiac Fiero of 1984 was unfortunately named. It became plagued by fears that it was a fire risk.
By summer 1987 there were reports of 20 fires a month involving the car. The National Highway Traffic Safety Administration received 149 complaints following fires, including six injuries. Experts estimate one in 508 of the cars caught fire due to a faulty con-rods in the engine. It caused oil leaks which ignited.
Pontiac tried to blame drivers for not checking their oil regularly. Then there was a mass recall in 1987 but the problem wasn't fixed.
By 1988 GM had reports of 260 Fiero fires with ten injuries and finally production was stopped.

314 Charity tycoon
Ratan Tata, the Indian chairman of Tata, which builds Jaguar, Land Rover and Tata vehicles, is one of the biggest philanthropists in the world.
He donates up to 65% of his huge income to charity projects. He has donated hundreds of millions to American academic institutions too and once gave US$50 million to Cornell University in New York, where he studied architecture, becoming the institution's biggest-ever donor.

315 Bentley business

Businessman John Bentley is a familiar site around Batley in Yorkshire, Northern England, in his vintage 1931 Bentley. "I didn't buy it because of my name, but now I have it everyone knows me as 'Bentley with the Bentley'. People make jokes about it, but the Bentley has become one of my business's best selling points." His company, Bentley Engineering, make car components.

316 Auto reverse

Industry experts have examined the technology and patents to speculate that Ford's future self-driving autonomous car will be able to repossess itself if owners fail to keep up payments.

317 Titanic car

When the world's most famous sinking happened – the Titanic in 1912 – there was a car on board. William Carter of Pennsylvania, USA had bought a new Renault Type CB Coupe de Ville while touring Europe with his wife and two children.
It was loaded into the liner's hold to be carried back to the US but sunk to the bottom of the Atlantic when the Titanic struck an iceberg. The Carters thankfully had a better voyage and all escaped the sinking.

318 Five alive

The French car brand built a special one-off electric version of its Renault 5 in 2022… to celebrate the 50th anniversary of the hatchback's launch.
The Renault Diamant was produced in collaboration with avantegarde French architect and designer Pierre Gonalons. The car's unusual specs include an external fingerprint scanner to open the door, horsehair fabrics and a fake-marble spiral-shaped steering wheel. The body is painted in gold flakes on top of a pink base.
The car is due to be auctioned to Renault enthusiasts at an undisclosed price.

319 Car confessions
A fifth of all male drivers have admitted using their car as a place to have sex.

320 Rechargers charged
Two thieves making a get-away in a Tesla Model X were caught when they had to stop to recharge it.
The robbers took $8,000-worth of electric items from a club in Georgia, USA in Spring 2023. Within ten miles however they had to stop to charge the car and were caught by police.

• In 2019 a woman who tried to steal a Tesla Model S in Arizona was caught when it ran out of charge as she tried to drive off.

• In 2020 a car-jacker was caught when he forced a driver from his Tesla Model 3 but the owner promptly locked the car with his phone App trapping the thief inside.

321 Super Jag
The 1992 Jaguar XJ220 was one of the first superfast supercars. It was powered by a twin-turbo V6 mounted in the middle of the low sleek two-door body. It was officially the world's fastest production car for a while after racing driver Martin Brundle took it to 217mph (349kph) on Italy's Nardo Track.
The XJ220 was also one the world's most expensive at the time. It cost around £470,000 (US$570,000) but Jaguar still managed to sell all the 275 cars it built.

322 Crossing point
Alice Ramsey became the first woman to drive across America in 1909. The 22-year-old pioneer was promoting a four-cylinder Maxwell car. Ramsey and her all female support team also showed women were able to handle the minor repairs and maintenance that such a journey entailed in those primitive early days of motoring.

323 Child spot
Nearly 10 per cent of drivers admit to having parked in a designated parent-and-child parking space (despite not having a child).

324 Car boss book
When colourful hard-selling former Ford and Chrysler boss Lee Iacocca wrote an autobiography in 1984 it was as successful as his car sales techniques had been.
The book 'Iacocca: An Autobiography' was America's best-selling non-fiction hardback book of both 1984 and 1985.
Iacocca donated all proceeds to medical charities.

325 Knob knowledge
A Brodie Knob is a small handle attached to the rim of a steering wheel.
The main purpose of the door-knob style attachment is to ease one-handed steering while the driver operates other controls with the other hand or is travelling in reverse.
Brodie knobs were popular fittings on trucks and tractors to enable greater turning power before power steering. Their main use today is still in large trucks, to allow simultaneous steering and operation of the radio or gearshift.
They are also used on forklifts, riding lawnmowers, and ice re-surfacers, where frequent sharp turning is required. The knob is also standard equipment on most modern farm and commercial tractors.
The device is often nicknamed a 'suicide knob' because it is so useless for controlling the wheel during an emergency. It is also often called a 'knuckle buster' because if the wheel spins rapidly the knob can hit the driver's knuckle, forearm or elbow. Perhaps worst of all, if the driver is wearing a long-sleeved shirt, the protruding knob can get caught in the sleeve's cuff.

326 Camera focus

Britain has one of the highest concentrations of speed cameras in the world. It has 7,000 cameras – that's 900 more than the whole of the USA.

Only Brazil, Italy and Russia have more. The UK's cameras record 1.74 million speeding incidents a year.

327 ...and the best performing cameras

Research in 2022 identified the UK's most successful speed cameras, ie: the ones that have photographed the most drivers who have then been prosecuted.

Amazingly, one single roadside camera stands out as the nation's star performer, with more than double the hits of its nearest rival.

Here is the top ten with the number of prosecution in the last 12 months:

1
On the A40 between Long Drive and Welland Gardens
49,050
Metropolitan Police

2
M25 Junction 7-16, Surrey
23,134
Surrey Police

3
M4 Junction 20-19, Bristol
18,317
Avon & Somerset Police

4
A5460 Narborough Road, Leicester, Junction with Fullhurst Avenue
16,634
Leicestershire Police

5
M6 Junction 1-4 (Northbound and Southbound)
15,410
Warwickshire Police

6
Garston Way/Dock Road, Liverpool
15,295
Merseyside Police

7
M5 Junction 4a-6, Birmingham
15,062
West Mercia Police

8
A282 Dartford Tunnel Approach Road
14,423
Kent Police

9
Lewes Road, Brighton, Junction with Coldean Lane
14,172
Sussex Police

10
M6 Junction 7 & 8 N/B, Birmingham
12,762
West Midlands Police

328 ...and false images
* French authorities meanwhile have installed 10,000 dummy speeding cameras around the country, in addition to the 5,000 real ones.

329 My name is Earl

Perhaps the least likely early motoring business pioneer was Major Charles Henry John Chetwynd-Talbot, 20th Earl of Shrewsbury, 20th Earl of Waterford, 5th Earl Talbot, who usually went under the name of Viscount Ingestre (a village in Staffordshire).

The top-hatted British aristocrat went to Eton College and inherited his wealth and titles aged just 16.

In 1902 the moustachioed Earl founded Clement-Talbot Ltd with some French associates and built the UK's first car factory in London's North Kensington. The attractive building still stands with his aristocratic crest carved above the front entrance (it also appeared on the cars' radiators).

The factory complex also included marble columns, gilded frescoes and stained glass windows. The Earl died in 1921.

The Talbot company continued to successfully make cars independently until 1934, when it became part of Rootes and was later reborn as the Sunbeam Talbot brand in 1938.

330 Name game

Researching British people with the same name as their car Top Gear journalists had several very near misses.

They found a Mrs Peugeot who drives a Renault, Mr Rover who drives a Diahatsu, and a Mr Audi who doesn't own a car at all.

Enthusiast Kate Aston-Martin of Manchester tried hard to join in. She changed her name to her favourite car brand by deed-poll, joined the owners club and dated a man who works at the Aston Martin factory. Sadly however she couldn't afford one of the cars.

331 Racer's trial

The winner of the world's first competitive motor race, the 1894 Paris to Rouen event, was colourful champagne exporter Albert Lemaitre.

He promptly began a new career as one of the world's first racing drivers, competing in numerous early races.

Tragically Albert then became involved in a celebrated French murder of 1906. When his wife tried to divorce him, he pleaded with her to change her mind. He failed, so then shot and killed her with a revolver. He then shot himself in the head.

Incredibly, after hospital treatment, he survived. But when he heard what had happened, his wife's lover shot and, in this instance, killed himself.

Bizarrely Albert was then tried for manslaughter but the jury acquitted the racing driver, because it was " a crime of passion". When the verdict was announced the court erupted into applause.

332 Prejudice conqueror

Nellie Goins was a pioneering black American female dragster racing driver from Indiana in the late sixties and early seventies.

Nicknamed 'Nitro Nellie' she battled prejudices and lack of sponsorship to drive a car nicknamed 'The Conqueror'. It was built by her husband and her family formed the pit crew. The Conqueror was based on a customised Mustang. It was capable of 215mph.

333 Head count

The European country with the most cars per head is Poland with 849 per thousand. The least cars per head is in North Macedonia, with just 205 cars per thousand people.

334 Ghost writer

The 13th version of the new Rolls Royce 40/50hp model, built in 1907, was finished in shiny aluminium and used as a demonstrator by the company.

It was given the nickname 'Silver Ghost' because of its ethereal looks and quietness.

The reliability of the car was then demonstrated – by driving it from London to Glasgow and back with various journalists on board. The Edwardian prestige car didn't just do the round trip of around 850 miles once... it did it in a continuous repetitive sequence 27 times.

* The press began calling all 40/50hp models 'Silver Ghosts' regardless of their colour – but it wasn't until 1925 that Rolls itself began using the distinctive name for its upmarket range. Since then however the company has introduced two other spooky model names: the Phantom and Wraith.

335 Auto park

The world's first driverless valet car park has opened at Stuttgart Airport in Germany. It is only available to owners of high-end Mercedes cars with advanced autonomous driving features.

They drop the car outside their terminal and then it uses an app to drive itself to the parking garage nearby.

336 Car kicks

Swedish soccer star Zlatan Ibrahimovic likes to buy himself a new supercar on his birthday. For his 38th in 2019 he bought himself a rare Ferrari Monza SP2 for £1.4m/$1.8m.

For his 40th in 2021 he paid £400,000 for an electric Ferrari Sf90. He didn't like it, so swapped it for a Daytona SP3 costing £1.7m.

Zlatan also has a Ferrari Enzo, 430 Spider, Lamborghini Urus, Maserati GranTurismo MC and Porsche Spyder.

However, when playing for Manchester United the star was a brand ambassador for Swedish company Volvo, so he drove to training in a rather more humble Volvo XC90.

337 Gas power

In summer 2023 Toyota launched the first racing car powered by liquid hydrogen.

338 'Till then

The earliest motorcars were steered with a tiller similar to a motorboat.

But in 1894 Alfred Vacheron entered the Paris-Rouen road race in a Panhard and he fitted a revolutionary new device: a steering wheel (he called it a 'Volant'.)

Competing against 20 rivals that were all tiller-controlled cars, Alfred's steering wheel car only managed to finish 11th.

Within four years however, many more advanced production cars were available with steering wheels instead of tillers.

Customers loved them and by the start of World War One in 1914 tillers had virtually disappeared.

339 Extra Rolls

Rolls Royce, now under the control of BMW, has established an extraordinary range of optional extras.

These include an individually customizable array of 1600 fibre optic 'stars' in the car's interior roof – or the facility to have your own initials, family crest or emblem embroidered throughout the cabin's interior trim.

Others may choose to have a complete leather floor instead of carpet, a blue illuminated 'Spirit of Ecstacy' bonnet statuette, Rolls Royce pen set in the glovebox or a bespoke wicker picnic hamper in the boot. Rolls can also be specified to come with mother-of-pearl inlays and handmade jewellery boxes.

* Rolls' latest options list features some pretty hi-tech equipment too. The 'Night Vision System' uses a discreet infrared camera in the grille to detect the body heat of pedestrians up to 300 metres away even in total darkness. At the touch of a button their thermal image is clearly shown on the central control screen, giving drivers plenty of time to slow down and pass safely.

340 Charging points
The best place to own an electric car in the UK is Milton Keynes according to researchers who found it has the most charging points per head of population (371 for 270,203 people). Meanwhile the northern city of Bolton is the worst – with only 24 chargers for a population of 288,248.

341 Volcanic porker
Porsche marketing department recently came up with a strange way to show off its 911 sports car. They fitted giant BF Goodrich off-road tyres then drove the two-door rear-engined road-going coupe 19,708ft/6,007m up the steep rocky slopes of Ojos del Salado in Chile… the world's highest volcano.

342 Figures of disinterest
Nearly two-thirds (63%) of drivers say a car is just 'a set of wheels that gets me from A to B' (59% men and 67% women).

343 Danish mash up
A Danish lorry driver was arrested after his load of potatoes spilled across a busy bridge near Copenhagen creating huge tailbacks as drivers tried to negotiate the potato-covered carriageway. Police said the roads became so slippery they were 'an endangerment to life.'

344 Survey avoidance
Another page, another survey. This time it's by motoring researchers at Zutobi who tried to find the worst countries to drive in.
Like other surveys they calculated price of fuel, risk of death, road quality and congestion. This time they came up with the world's worst country to drive in being: Israel.
Runners-up in this avoidance list were Argentina, Columbia, Chile and Peru.

345 Mall practice
A Florida woman was arrested after she left her children in the car while she went on a shoplifting spree in a mall.
While she was gone for over an hour her Lincoln burst into flames and the children were rescued by other shoppers and taken to hospital with burns.

346 Reach for the stars
When Alan Astra of Stevenage, UK, bought a Vauxhall Astra, the manufacturer gave him a free tour of its Ellesmere Port factory where it is made. He's a professional magician and bought the Astra because he says "people expect something special when you are an entertainer."
Because of his name he is famous at his local garage. "All of them know me and say 'here comes Mr Astra and his Astra'. I like it, it helps people remember me. And besides, the estate comes in handy for carting my props around."

347 Stag chests
Meanwhile engineer Barry Stagg of Cornwall, UK, is the only member of the Triumph Stag owners club with the same name as his car. Sadly at the time of being interviewed the 1970 car was in pieces kept in tea chests in his neighbour's garage.

348 Fatal service
Tragically an 11-month-old baby girl died after being left unattended in hot car for three hours… while her parents went to a church service in Palm Bay, Florida in 2023.

349 Race apart

The world's first competitive motor race in 1894 between Paris and Rouen (76 miles/122km) boasted the massive prize money of 10,000 francs. Because of this huge amount, the event attracted a bizarre selection of entrants. A total of 102 vehicles paid ten francs to enter.

Many competitors featured strange untried technologies: five claimed to use 'compressed air' power, there was a 'gravity-powered' engine, a car that ran on oil and another that ran on 'gas'. One competing vehicle claimed to be 'powered by pedals', another used a mysterious system described as 'levers' and there was a 'baricycle' that attempted to move by "the weight of its passengers".

Perhaps unsurprisingly 78 of these entries didn't turn up for qualifying and were never heard of again.

Among those that did turn up, the race was won by a French nobleman wearing a bowler hat.

However Marquis Jules Felix Philippe Albert de Dion de Wandonne's steam-powered car was promptly disqualified on the sort of technicality that has dogged motor racing ever since. Dion's car was booted out because it was deemed not 'easy to drive'. That was because it required a coal stoker to operate the steam boiler.

First prize was instead then awarded to a more conventional petrol-powered Peugeot.

350 Sound action

A network of 'sound cameras' has been installed in Central London to catch drivers whose exhausts are too loud. The devices in Kensington and Chelsea have already registered 10,000 culprits exceeding the legal limit of noise (76dB). The commonest car culprits are BMW, followed by Lamborghini, Mercedes, Ferrari, Audi and Land Rover. The noisy car owners risk a £100 fine.

351 Bird spotting

The unusually-named 1930 Humber Snipe, and later the longer Super Snipe, were British luxury saloons. The name is taken from a type of small mottled-brown wading bird.

352 Fast news
In November 2022 the Croatian supercar, the Rimac Nevera, set a new record speed for a production electric vehicle: 258mph (412kph). The US$2.1million EV set the record at the steeply banked Papenburg test track in Germany.
At the time of writing the speed record for a petrol car is held by the Shelby SSC Tuatara at 282.9mph (455kph).

353 Memorial day
The first gasoline-powered vehicle available for sale in the United States was a three-wheel invention called the Buckeye Buggy in 1891. It was built and marketed by inventor John William Lambert of Ohio.
The Lambert Days Festival happens every July in Ohio to celebrate his achievement. It includes sports events, art festivals and of course a car show.

354 Clio clues
Pierre and Sheila Renault of Ivybridge, Devon, UK, own a Renault Clio, their fourth car to share their name.
Pierre is a distant relative of the founder of the French marque.
"It causes problems when I take it in for service," says Sheila, "they write down what the car is, then ask for your name. I say 'Renault' and they say 'we've already got the car name thank you madam' and they think you're stupid. But we're really quite happy with our Clio."

355 Hyper EV
A hypercar concept unveiled at New York Motor Show in 2022 claims to be the most powerful ever.
The Vayanne, produced by Deus Automobiles in Austria, (with help from Ital Design and Williams Engineering) is an exotic-looking all-electric coupe with a claimed 2,200bhp.
The 0-60 sprint takes less than two seconds and top speed is around 250mph (400kph). Unfortunately a production version of the car hadn't been launched – and still hasn't appeared at the time of writing.

356 Aston's value

An immaculate maroon completely standard Aston Martin DB5 sports saloon that had only covered 27,000 miles since being bought for £4,248 in 1964 sold for £506,000 at auction in 2022.

357 Oriental tyres

The world's largest full-size tyre manufacturer is Bridgestone. The company doesn't sound it – but is Japanese.
It was founded in 1931 by local businessman Shojiro Ishibashi. Ishibashi means 'stone bridge' in Japanese, hence the name Bridgestone.

358 Duelling Dion

Pioneering auto engineer and racing driver Jules Félix Philippe Albert de Dion de Wandonne, who finished first in the world's first competitive car race, was an eccentric French nobleman. The colourful Marquis was briefly jailed for hitting the French President with his walking stick at the Auteuil horse-racing track in 1899. De Dion's excuse was that he disgreed with the President.
The Marquis was notorious for fighting duels too. An early black-and-white photograph shows the President of the French Automobile Club sword fighting against French socialist politician and journalist Alfred Gerault-Richard. The 1902 duel was believed to be the last fought in Paris. Incredibly it lasted an hour – until De Dion wounded his opponent's arm and the fight was abandoned. "No reconciliation occurred" reported contemporary newspapers.
His name has been preserved among motoring history as a type of suspension system called the de Dion axle. The duelling Marquis was given the credit but did not design it. It was instead created by his brother-in-law Charles Trepardoux, who appeared not to contest the naming of the device with his ferocious relative.

359 Not MOT
One in ten British drivers admit to having driven illegally without the mandatory annual MOT test certificate. A survey by car insurers found that the biggest MOT-dodgers are in Liverpool, followed by Cardiff, Leeds and Norwich.

360 Safe haven
I've half mentioned this already, but it seems the safest place to drive in Europe is Switzerland. It has a road traffic death rate of just 1.71 per 100,000 people.
Take care in Bosnia however, it has the highest road death rate at 10.79 per 100,000... that's more than ten times for dangerous than Switzerland.

361 Exclusive options
Maybach buyers are offered exclusive optional extras including granite trim or golden keys. Ultra-rich customers who select Maybach's perfume atomizer, built-in printer, reclining rear seats with built in massage pads and fridge with silver champagne flutes are probably merely adding design touches that they already have in their homes (and their boats).
* A special edition Hermès Bugatti launched recently features door handles resembling those of Hermès luggage. Buyers also get a bespoke, hand-made travel bag in the leather-lined boot and a dashboard glove compartment designed to precisely fit a Hermès wallet.

362 Big wheels
Early Formula One cars used large wooden steering wheels taken straight from road cars. They had as large a diameter as possible, to reduce the effort needed to turn the front wheels.

363 Road density
The European country with the least roads is Iceland, with just 13 kms of road per 1,000 square kms of land mass. Belgium has the most roads, with 388 km of tarmac in every 1,000 square kms.

364 Wrong gear

Volvo's first ever car rolled proudly out of the new company's workshop in Sweden in 1927.

The men building the first model of the Jakob four-seater had made a huge error however – they'd put the rear axles on the wrong way round. This meant the car had one forward gear... and four reverse ones.

The car had to immediately return to the workshop to be rebuilt.

365 Sports tent

Luxury sportscar maker Porsche has released the most unlikely extra for its 911 supercar: a tent containing a mattress that sits on top of the car.

For around 5,000 Euros the 'roof tent' upgrade is pneumatically powered to inflate at the touch of a button. It includes a fold-up ladder, rain-cover with windows and 6.9ft foam mattress. A heated blanket is available at extra cost. Some 911s are capable of over 200mph (322kph) but owners who opt for the roof tent are limited to just 80mph (130kph).

366 Will power

Victorian cloth-maker William Riley switched to making bicycles when times got hard. At the same time he also managed to have five sons, all of which he confusingly christened William too. The five are now known by their middle names: Percy, Stanley, Victor, Allan and Cecil.

Between them all they created the Riley Car Company, which grew to become one of Britain's most successful car-makers. It built cars from 1890 to 1969.

The Riley brand is now owned by BMW.

367 Name games

A car-parts delivery driver from Peterborough, England, called Anna Citroen spends all day at the wheel of a Citroen C15 van. Meanwhile Mollie Hillman of Dorset, UK, owns a 1958 Hillman Minx Convertible. "Everyone thinks we bought it for the name," she says, "but really we just wanted a convertible so our sick poodle could get some fresh air as we drove along."

368 The little big three

In post-war Britain three motoring brands fought a fierce battle for market leadership.

Dinky, Corgi and Matchbox sold millions of toy cars at pocket-money prices, competing fiercely with features like doors that opened, suspension that worked and wheels that steered.

Corgi took the lead for a while after the huge success of its James Bond Aston Martin DB5 featuring miniaturised gadgets from the film car, including an ejector seat.

The big three little car-makers battled to attract collectors with detailed catalogues and wide ranges covering every type of vehicle, from sports cars to steamrollers.

In the seventies the Hong Kong-made Hot Wheels series arrived and sent the market into a spin. Hot Wheels were cheaper, gaudier and had much more freely spinning wheels. They were less of a model, more of a plaything.

Hot Wheels took over leadership of the toy market briefly – but at the same time the arrival of cheap playthings signalled the end of the metal model car era.

369 The Ford show

In 1953 Ford celebrated its 50th anniversary by taking over prime-time American TV for two whole hours. Ford paid an enormous fee to broadcast a show called The American Road on both NBC and CBS, uninterrupted by commercial breaks.

The programme featured music, comedy and features with a cast of stars including Bing Crosby, Frank Sinatra and a recitation of Winston Churchill's 'Finest Hour' speech.

There were clips of the Model T Ford in silent movies and as a grand finale Henry Ford II made a speech about America's potential for the future.

370 Snow business

Hollywood actor Jeremy Renner who plays Marvel superhero was hospitalised after running himself over at his home in Nevada, USA. The 'Hawkeye' super-archer character was badly injured when he was run over by his own heavy-duty snowplough early in 2023.

The multi-millionaire actor had jumped from the plough to move a car stuck in the snow – but his tracked vehicle had continued to roll along and ran right over its owner.

371 Victorian cats

The first catalytic converters to remove toxic material from car exhausts were fitted to French cars in the late 1800s. They were experimental metal cylinders lined with clay containing platinum, rhodium and palladium.

The first automotive catalytic converters in the US weren't produced and fitted for a further 80 years.

372 Fastest food

A survey in 2022 found that 98.5% of UK service stations have a fast-food counter. Out of the 127 motorway services only eight have a fresh food counter. Costa, Burger King and Greggs are the most common outlets.

* The Gloucester motorway services on the M5 has been judged the UK's healthiest. It has a farm shop, butchers, cheese shop and deli. It even sells fresh fish. There are no fast-food stores in the service station at all.

373 New string to his bow

Violinist Frank Marugg was the unlikely inventor of the car wheel-clamp.

The professional classical musician played with the Denver Symphony Orchestra in the fifties and befriended many local police chiefs. They were looking for a new solution to parking problems in the city and Marugg dreamt up a locking wheel clamp system still called the Denver Boot in America.

The city police started using Marugg's device in January 1955 and used it to collect over US$18,000 in its first month in use (that's worth almost $250,000 today).

Over the next 15 years Marugg sold thousands of the devices and his daughter carried on the business making and selling clamps until 1986.

374 Nazi driving school

The NSKK, The National Socialist Motor Corps, was part of the German Nazi organisation whose members were screened for pure Aryan racial traits.

Its prime aim was teaching "fitness in motoring skills". All German racing drivers had to join the organisation and by the outbreak of World War Two it had trained around 200,000 drivers.

375 Secret supervans

In 1971 Ford engineers constructed a one-off promotional 'Supervan' based on a normal white Ford Transit but powered by the Le Mans-winning 435bhp GT40 engine mounted just behind the seats.

In 2022 they produced another madly over-powered promotional white Transit Supervan for the Goodwood Festival of Speed. The Ford Custom Transit comes with a side door and useable rear load areas but was also fitted with a monstrous 1,973bhp of AWD electric power. Four electric motors powered the light commercial vehicle from 0-62mph (0-100kph) in less than two seconds making it probably the fastest commercial vehicle ever made.

376 Seeing the light
Academic researchers studied data from thousands of streets across 62 local authority areas on the UK spanning ten years – and found that car crime FALLS if there are no street lights. Residents had campaigned against council plans to save money by turning lights off after midnight but the study found that there are more thefts of and from vehicles in brightly-lit streets. Researchers speculated that it is because thieves can better see what they are doing.

377 Running time
Runabouts were a popular style of car in America in the 1910s. A runabout was a light and inexpensive vehicle with no windscreen, doors or side windows. It had a convertible hood, two seats and four small wheels. This genre included the Oldsmobile Curved Dash, Gale Runabout and the Cadillac Runabout.

378 Motor maker
Honda is the world's largest producer of internal combustion engines, building more than 14 million a year.

379 Cost to race
The average annual cost of running a Formula One racing team is estimated to be around £220,000,000/$265,000,000 – roughly a quarter of a billion pounds.

380 Leyland Lord

Leonard Lord was not an aristocrat as his name implies. In fact the Times once called him a "foul-mouthed, hard driving production man."

Lord ran Austin from 1941, combined it with Morris to create the British Motor Corporation – and then died in 1967 as he was negotiating the mergers that would unify the UK motor industry as British Leyland.

He was from a humble Coventry family and had left school at 16 to train as a draughtsman. Lord worked in engineering works and factories, eventually excelling his way to the top of Morris Motors.

He fell out dramatically with William Morris and stormed out of the Morris complex in Oxford famously threatening to "take Cowley apart, brick by brick".

When he took over at Austin, Lord introduced a worldwide motoring vision and set up factories in Canada, Australia, Argentina, South Africa and Mexico. He later amalgamated with Morris and had to work with William, then Lord Nuffield, once more.

Lord has been criticised for overseeing the decline of the British motor industry but other motor historians point out he had the vision to employ Alec Issigonis to create the Mini, unified disparate failing manufacturers and updated a desperately old-fashioned industry.

In 1962 he was made a lord to match his name and became Baron Lambury. With no son, the hereditary title disappeared when he died.

381 Radioactive sparks

Between 1940 and 1953 Firestone made and sold 'Supreme' sparkplugs made from radioactive polonium. The radioactivity wasn't a secret – it marketed as a benefit because it was considered a boost to performance.

382 Baby alarm

An Australian tech company has launched the 'Infalurt' device – to warn drivers they have forgotten there is a baby in their car.

The system is a solution to increasing incidents where drivers have got out of their car, forgetting there is a baby in safety seat in the back and left it there.

An alarm is set off in the key fob if the driver is detected to be more than 10m/30ft from the car while a baby is in a monitored child seat. The system costs AUD$369 (about US$273/£225).

383 Monster mash

In 2010 a Swedish device was launched that plugged into a car cigarette lighter and made the engine sound like a monster V8 truck.

384 Quick work

The speedometer was invented by Josip Belusic, a Croatian engineer, in 1888. He presented it at a World Fair in Paris and called the new device a 'velocimeter'.

It was the world's first monitoring device – of any kind.

385 Six Maseratis

In the late 19th century Italian train-driver Rodolfo Maserati and wife Carolina had six sons – who combined forces to create the Maserati car company.

386 Drive-through pranks

After the hashtag #Drivethruprank accumulated more than 550 million views on TikTok, researchers (who on earth paid them this time?) found the top six most popular practical jokes that have been filmed at the world's drive-through take-aways.

Stolen Food Prank
The most popular 'joke' on the hashtag is the stolen food prank. Here a customer attempts to get their food order twice. As the customer is handed their food, an accomplice on foot who has been hiding around the corner runs up and grabs the food, confusing the poor service workers.

Wrong Food Prank
The customer goes to another fast food restaurant first, like KFC for example, then heads to McDonalds with a rival burger. Once the customer is handed their order, they replace the McDonald's with KFC and claim they were given the wrong food.

Disappearing Food Prank
The disappearing food prank can easily confuse workers. Tricksters quickly hide the order under the car seat and claim the bag they were given was empty. A viral version of this prank sees a customer go as far to pour a drink down the inside of his top, then claim the cup was given to him empty.

Kissing Prank
A couple order food and as they are about to be handed the order, they begin kissing non-stop. The worker trying to hand them the order is completely ignored by the passionate couple. In one viral video the service gives up trying and shuts the window on them.

Fake Speaker Prank
This elaborate prank involves a fake speaker box fitted with a walkie-talkie ahead of the actual drive-thru ordering spot. When customers approach it and try to make an order, the prankster sitting in the car park will humiliate and trick other customers over the walkie-talkie. One viral hit sees a prankster convince a customer to reverse back through a KFC drive-thru to get free food, telling him to "back up for a bucket."

Invisible Driver Prank
The invisible driver prank takes the most pre-planning. A driver camouflages themselves by folding the seat down but covering themselves with a coloured cardboard structure matching the seat fabric. The driver seems completely invisible. One video shows a service worker extremely confused as the invisible customer shouts "just throw it (the food) in here, I'm a ghost."

387 Time line
When Henry Ford installed a production line system at his car factory it cut the average time for making a car from 12.5 hours to 1.5 hours.

* Ford concentrated on black paintjobs at the time because it dried faster than other colours.

388 A Princess's passion

King Charles' sister Princess Anne is a big fan of the obscure brand of Scimitar cars.

The first one she ever owned was more than half a century ago when she was given an Air Force blue 1970 GTE, as a joint 20th birthday and Christmas present from her parents, Queen Elizabeth and Prince Philip.

The Scimitar was at the time a niche sporting estate produced by Reliant.

The range used fibreglass bodies and Ford engines and appeared in various forms between 1964 and 1986. Reliant was based in the small town of Tamworth in Staffordshire in England's Midlands.

Since her original Scimitar, the Royal Princess has added another eight Scimitars to her collection. All her models have the same registration number as the original vehicle: 1420 H.

389 Big family

The Stellantis multinational motor manufacturing corporation, based in Amsterdam, The Netherlands, currently sells 16 different brands of vehicle:

Abarth, Alfa Romeo, Chrysler, Citroen, Dodge, DS, Fiat, Fiat Professional, Jeep, Lancia, Maserati, Mopar, Opel, Peugeot, Ram and Vauxhall.

390 Board members

In the early 20th century all cars were fitted with running boards. There were flat steps that ran the length of the body and helped people step up into the car's cabin. They were occasionally used by passengers to sit or stand on.

A famous image of running boards would be inter-war armed American gangsters standing like guards on the running boards of their bosses' cars.

The first car without a running board was believed to be the Ruxton in 1929 but it wasn't until 1936 that a top-selling model, the Cord, made the lack of running boards fashionable.

391 Morris lungs

The founder of Morris Cars, William Morris was a noted philanthropist. In 1938 he commissioned the building of 1700 of the latest 'iron lung' respirator machines on his car assembly lines and donated them to hospitals all over Britain and the Commonwealth.

392 Backward progress

In the 1950s all General Motors cars with automatic gearboxes arranged the 'R' for reverse right next to 'L' for low forward gear. There followed a spate of accidents where drivers accidentally went forwards instead of backwards. To make it worse the drivers were turning round looking out the rear window expecting to reverse as they shot forwards. American authorities had introduced standardised automatic gear patterns by the end of the decade. From then on the PRNDL system kept R and L safely apart.

393 Nazi champion

German racing driver Rudolf Caracciola was a member of a Nazi Paramilitary Group when he won the European Drivers' Championship an unsurpassed three times in 1935, 1937 and 1938.

394 Cool choices

A poll by motoring magazine AutoExpress in 2023 found the 'coolest cars in the world'.

They are:
1 Citroen DS
2 Jaguar E-Type
3 Lancia Stratos
4 Land Rover Defender
5 Lamborghini Miura
6 Mini (original)
7 Lotus Esprit
8 Porsche 911
9 Audi Quattro
10 McLaren F1
11 Ferrari 288 GTO
12 Mercedes 280 SL Pagoda
13 VW Golf GTI
14 Fiat 500
15 Range Rover Classic
16 Alfa Romeo Spider
17 BMW M3 (1986)
18 Ford Capri
19 Nissan Skyline
20 Toyota 2000GT

395 Worldwide web

In 2014 Mazda was forced to recall 42,000 models of its popular 6 series model for a repair – because of spiders. The company had discovered that the car engine was particularly vulnerable to webs created by the yellow sac spider, which is attracted to the smell of petrol. Their webs can cause blockages leading to fires in the engine.

An attempt to fit covers to prevent the spiders gaining access failed – so Mazda had to resort to a free software update for owners that warned drivers of any new blockages in the fuel system.

The New York Times asked for more explanation at the time but a Mazda spokesman replied: "Don't ask me, I'm terrified of the damned things."

* Subaru had to recall all recent cars for an urgent fix to its 'Audiovox' remote engine start system. The company discovered that if the owner's fob was dropped it could accidentally transmit an engine start message to the car – which would then automatically start and run for 15 minutes.

396 Listen for clues

One of the strangest bits of promotional research among dozens in this book must be this one that came from the UK's Admiral Insurance company.

It tested 1,000 motorists to see how well they could recognise unusual noises made by a car that each signify various mechanical problems. Examples are squeaky noise of a failing water pump and the ominous click-then-silence of a dead battery.

The results of this strange report show that the over 65s are best at identifying faults from the noises and millennials are the worst. Drivers from the northeast were the best at the tests, drivers from London were the worst.

The easiest noise to identify was trying to start a car with a dead battery, followed by the engine seizing up and pistons slapping.

The hardest to spot was the water pump squeak, followed by a vacuum hose leak and a bad ball joint.

At the time of writing these strange tests are still live online so if the pages stay up there you can have a go at it too: https://www.admiral.com/guides/motor/sound-of-motors#home

397 Pole position

Little known Polish engineer Alfred Rzeppa emigrated to America and started working for Ford Motor Company. There he invented and patented the constant-velocity joint in 1926. The ingenious way of transferring power across different angles has since been a major part of automotive mechanical engineering.

398 Autonomous ski bus

One of the best autonomous transport ideas yet devised must be the dolaGon Ski Lift Vehicle. It has been designed by American skiing-mad surgeon Dr Seth Neubardt.
The good doc has modified a Polaris Ranger UTV with tracks instead of wheels and added extra tech like radar sensors and GPS. Now the dolaGon takes up to six skiers on a pre-defined backcountry route to the top of a mountain, drops them off – and while they ski down it makes its own way back down to pick them up again, using GPS to find them and radar to avoid bumping into trees.

399 Ticket escapes

Around one-in-six of UK speeding tickets are later cancelled, repealed or ignored.

Fifth gear
From Clarkson's embarrassment…
to The End

400 Waist wait
During filming of the 2023 series of Grand Tour, presenter
Jeremy Clarkson was trapped in the cockpit of a Formula One
racing car.
The 63-year-old TV star was hoping to race co-presenters
Richard Hammond and James May around Poznan race track
in Poland but became trapped by his large waistline.
Observers report that he had to wait in embarrassment as the
body of the car was dismantled around the cockpit to release
him.

401 Rail disaster
The founder of MG Cars, Cecil Kimber, was killed in the
famous tragic King's Cross railway accident of 1945. His first
class compartment was crushed as the carriage was derailed
and crashed into a signal gantry. The motoring boss was 56.

402 Dash debut
The word dashboard originates from the barrier fitted at the
front of a horse-drawn carriage to protect occupants from mud
'dashed-up' by the horses' hooves.
The early horseless carriages retained this board to protect
passengers from debris thrown up by the front wheels. This
was a convenient place to mount instruments and controls –
so that's where the modern dashboard started.

403 Caviar car

Bugatti's new special edition Veyron is leading the way in performance, price… and bedazzling extras. The latest special edition, for example, the exclusive £1.5 million, 253mph L'Or Blanc model, is distinguished by ample use of fine German porcelain on details like the fuel cap, wheel badges and even a caviar tray to sit on the centre console.

404 Touch line

A 53-year-old Liverpool man was given an unusual court order in 2023: he was banned from touching any parking meters in the city for two years. The 'punishment' came after a conviction for stealing from a parking machine.

405 Conquest commemoration

The new Daimler saloon launched in 1953 was called The Conquest. It was no coincidence that the car cost exactly £1066 – the date of the famous Battle of Hastings and the Norman Conquest.

406 Electric sequence

Electric cars are nothing new of course… in fact the first land speed record was broken in 1898 by an electric car, travelling at the ungodly haste of 39mph/63kph. The following five LSRs were all set by electric cars too. Their sequence of records was eventually broken, at a hair-raising 75mph/121kph… by a steam car.

407 Samsung cars

Japanese high-tech phone and appliance maker Samsung decided to form an offshoot to start making cars in 1994. It was just starting to sell its products by 1998 when Asia was hit by a sudden financial crisis – and the fledgling Samsung car company was promptly taken over by Renault.

408 Hitler's cars

Adolf Hitler loved cars and had a famous collection – even though he never learned to drive. When he committed suicide in Berlin in 1945 the petrol tanks of his car collection were drained – to burn his body so it could not be recognised.

409 Lambo tractor

The R8 is the fastest, flashiest Audi sports car – and the name of Lamborghini's biggest farm tractor. TV presenter Jeremy Clarkson bought an R8 tractor for his farm because he thought it would be faster but it turned out to be too big for his barn.

* Porsche also produced tractors in the fifties and sixties.

410 Top lots

The ten most expensive cars ever sold at auction
(from Jalopnik.com in 2022 – but these sort of lists change all the time)

1 Mercedes 300 SLR Uhlenhaut Coupe
US$143,000,000 (£117m)
This 1955 two-door, three-litre sports coupe was based on Juan Manual Fangio's World Championship-winning Grand Prix car. It was specially designed to win the World Sportscar Championship – which it did. It was capable of 180mph (290kph).
It was sold in 2022 at an exclusive auction held at the Mercedes Museum in Stuttgart, Germany, to "a private collector".

2 Ferrari 250 GTO
US$48,405,000 (£39.6m)
Sold by Sotheby's in 2018, this 1962 red sports racing coupe was only the third GTO ever built and is often quoted as the most-expensive car ever (but it no longer is).

3 Ferrari 250 GTO Berlinetta
US$38,115,000 (£31.2m)

Another 1962 red GTO but it's a different car. It was the 19th GTO built (only 36 were made). The three-litre V12-powered coupe was last sold at Bonhams in 2014 having been previously owned by the same family for 49 years.

4 Ferrari 335S
US$35,730,510 (£29.2m)
Another red Ferrari – this time it's a 1956 open-top two-seater. The 335S is very rare, one of just four that were made. It was sold at auction for more than £29 million in 2016. Incidentally, the 335S was insanely fast for the era. It can do a seriously swift 186mph (300kph).

5 Mercedes W196R
US$29,600,000 (£24.2m)
This iconic single-seat racer from 1954 marked Germany's return to Grand Prix racing after the war. It was another car driven by Fangio to win the world title. Only 14 were built. Ten survive and Mercedes owns six of them. This one was sold in 2013.

6 Ferrari 290MM
US$28,050,000 (£22.9m)
Someone paid $28 million for this 1956 open-top Ferrari when it was auctioned in 2015. It was actually built for good-old Fangio again – and is one of just four made.

7 Ferrari 275 GTB/4*S NART Spider
US$27,500,000 (£22.5m)
Catchy name. The pretty 1967 Spider with a V12 engine sold in 2013 at Sotheby's.
The NART bit refers to it being one of ten built for the North American market.

8 Ferrari 275 GTB/C Speciale
US$26,400,000 (£21.6m)
This 1964 V12 coupe is actually grey, not red. That didn't stop someone paying more than $26 million for the two-door hardtop coupe at Sotheby's in 2014.

9 Aston Martin DBR1
US$22,550,000 (£18.4m)
The first of five DBR1s built in 1956, this low-slung green open-top sportster has a great heritage, including being raced by Stirling Moss, Carroll Shelby and Jack Brabham. It came complete with a spare engine when it sold in 2017.

10 Ferrari 290MM
US$22,005,000 (£18m)
Another 1956 290MM – a red open-top classic sports racing car. This is the last one built and sold at auction in 2018.

411 Re-test over-70s
More than 60 per cent of UK drivers believe that driving retests for the over 70s should be made mandatory. In the 18-34 age group, this number rose to over 75%, while only 42% of over 55s agree with the idea.

412 Small collection
Miniature Russian social media star Hasbulla is just 3ft 4in tall but has amassed a car collection that he is too small to drive. It includes a Mercedes G-Wagen, Ram Rebel TRX and BMW M5.
The favourite of the dwarfism sufferer, however, is a custom-made miniature Ford Shelby Cobra small enough for him to reach the pedals.

413 Budd's bazookas
Former Philadelphia machine-shop apprentice Edward G Budd became an expert on making steel. In 1912 he founded the Budd Company. Within a year had convinced the Dodge brothers to purchase 70,000 all-steel open-top car bodies from him. Budd's business thrived and during the Second World War it built bazookas for the Allies.

414 Shark tale
Every new Vauxhall and Opel car produced since 2004
features a secret moulding somewhere on the car containing
the shape of a shark. It could be anywhere, like on the
glovebox door or under the cupholders.
The tradition has continued under new owner Stellantis. The
company explains why: "One Sunday in 2004, Opel designer
Dietmar Finger (that REALLY is his name) was at home
drawing a design for the new Corsa. More precisely, the
unspectacular outer wall of the glove box, which is covered
most of the time by the closed passenger door. When the box
is opened, this wall must provide stability, which is achieved
with transverse ribs in the plastic surface. The designer now
had to design these ribs. As he was in the middle of his
design, his son walked by, took a look at the sketch and
asked: "Dad, why don't you draw a shark?" Why not? Finger
thought to himself and gave the ribs the shape of a shark. An
idea and a new tradition was born."

415 Common complaints
The most common grumbles of British motorists were revealed
in a survey in 2022. The list of gripes included:
72% put off electric vehicles by the cost
58% considering there are not enough charging points
80% not trusting driverless cars
71% claiming potholes are the biggest issue on British roads
60% believe fuel duty should be reduced
58% believe fuel companies make too higher profits

416 Spreading light
In 1947 Zippo lighters built a giant motorised model of its flip-
top lighter based on the underpinnings of a Chrysler New
Yorker. The promotional vehicle was then driven to all 48
contiguous states of America.

417 Normal Royal

A standard 2013 Baltic Blue Range Rover Vogue SE belonging to the British Royal Household and driven by Prince William and Kate the Duchess of Cambridge sold at auction for £50,625 in 2022, a price which was not far from its normal re-sale value.

418 All for show

The majority of UK car owners (76%) buy their car from a car showroom, because:

34% wish to part-exchange their vehicle
33% want a showroom warranty - this is particularly important for over 66s (41%), compared to under 34s (25%)
21% like a showroom's after-sales service
11% want to be able to access finance options
In contrast, almost one in ten (9%) prefer to buy a car online or privately so they don't have to deal with car salespeople (10% men and 8% women) and 12% say they can get a better deal not buying through a showroom.
The remaining buyers purchase cars from a private seller (9%), car supermarkets (4%), online retailers (3%) and gifts from family members (3%).

* One in twenty (5%) drivers are happy to buy a car online without even seeing it (8% men and 3% women), rising to one in ten (11%) under 34s, compared to 4% of over 55s. And 9% would also buy a car without a test drive (11% men and 6% women).

419 Monster sounds

The new Lotus Eletre all-electric SUV features a monstrous 2,160-watt sound system with 23 KEF speakers.

420 Famous faces

The Automotive Hall of Fame is a museum honouring influential figures in the history of the motor industry. It stands in the heart of America's car manufacturing home of Dearborn, Michigan.

When founded in 1939 it was called the "Automobile Old Timers'.

At the latest count there are 271 inductees including: Giovanni Agnelli, Mario Andretti, W.O. Bentley, Bertha Benz, Karl Benz, Nuccio Bertone, Attore Bugatti, David Buick, Louis Chevrolet, Walter Chrysler, Andre Citroen, Gottlieb Daimler, Rudolf Diesel, Horace Dodge, John Dodge, Fred Duesenberg, John Dunlop, William Durant, Thomas Edison, Harvey Firestone, Edsel Ford, Henry Ford, Henry Ford II, Giorgetto Giugiaro, Dan Gurney, Donald Healey, Phil Hill, Soichiro Honda, Lee Iacocca, Alec Issigonis, Ferruccio Lamborghini, Jay Leno, Wilhelm Maybach, Andre Michelin, Edouard Michelin, Ralph Nader, Ransom Olds, Wilhelm Opel, James Ward Packard, William Doud Packard, Armand Peugeot, Ferdinand Piech, Sergio Pininfarina, Ferdinand Porsche, Louis Renault, Frederick Henry Royce, Carroll Shelby, Jackie Stewart, John Studebaker, Ratan Tata, Eiji Toyoda, Kiichiro Toyoda, Shoichiro Toyoda, and Preston Tucker.

421 Quiet job

Car exhaust silencers were invented in 1902 – by American inventor Percy Maxim who was actually trying to invent silencers for guns. Maxim's father had previously invented the machine gun and hair-curling irons.

422 Herr in a hurry

Acclaimed German racing car engineer Rudolf Uhlenhaut designed the fastest road car of the mid-fifties, the Mercedes SLR. It was said to be capable of astonishing speeds for the era: 180mph/290kph.

One day Uhlenhaut was in Munich and found he was late for a meeting in Stuttgart. The life-long motor engineer was said to have never owned a car.

So he borrowed one of the company's SLRs and roared along the autobahn, completing the 137-mile (220km) journey in just over an hour. Today that intercity journey normally takes over two-and-a-half hours.

423 Brain drain

Research published in the Proceedings of the National Academy of Sciences in America estimates that lead poisoning from car exhausts reduced the IQ of about half the population of the US in the sixties and seventies. The research claims some people were so damaged by the lead in fuel they lost around six per cent of their IQ.

424 The car upstairs

The woman driver of a white Subaru SUV lost control so badly at high speed that it left the road, flew 75 feet and crashed into the upstairs bedroom of a house. The car was left embedded in the second-storey of a shocked pensioner's home in Cofax, California, in summer 2023. The driver was taken to hospital for treatment.

425 Test errors

A study by Britain's Driver and Vehicle Standards Agency found than around one in seven vehicles that pass their annual MOT test should actually have failed. The DVSA sampled 1,700 vehicles after their MOT test. Around three in a hundred that failed should have passed.

426 Car smell

The 2023 one-off Rolls Royce Phantom Syntopia was produced with the help of Dutch fashion designer Iris van Verpen. It features a bespoke scent throughout the interior. The scent is described as a mix of cedarwood, iris, leather, rose with a hint of lemon.

427 Nose job

International motorsport's official governing body, the Federation International de l'Automobile mounted a full tear-long investigation into one of the serious apparent rule contraventions that was potentially harming the noble sport of Formula One racing: Lewis Hamilton's nose piercing.
After spending much of the 2022 season consulting with their medical team and trying to ban the seven-time-world-champion's nose stud, officials published a written verdict revealing "no further action will be taken" because of concerns that repeated removal of "the device" will lead to permanent disfigurement.

428 Polar power

The first car in Antarctica was a 1907 Arrol-Johnston powered by an alcohol-fuelled engine imported by a British expedition. The car got stuck in the snow and overheated.
After several other vehicle failures a humble VW Beetle proved to be a great success for a sixties Australian expedition. Its simple engineering and air-cooled engine made it dependable. The Beetle's light weight meant it rarely got stuck and could be easily lifted out if it did.
The red 'Antactica 1' Beetle became something of a major celebrity vehicle down-under. After serving its time on the ice continent it returned to take part in the 1964 Australian Rally – which it won.

429 Ford town

In the 1920s Henry Ford wanted to safeguard his supplies of rubber from the Amazon forest – so he built a town for Brazilian workers there. He called Fordlandia.

It was designed to house 10,000 people but was a disaster from the start. The site had no roads, was beset by tropical diseases and ignorance of local conditions. Workers were banned from having alcohol, tobacco or women, even in their own homes.

In 1930 there was a revolt that had to be quelled by the Brazilian army and in 1934 Fordlandia was abandoned.

It has only had a few dozen residents in the last 50 years and industry sources say that not once drop of rubber from the town ever made it to a Ford vehicle.

430 Charge point

A Chevy Bolt EV was quietly charging normally at a public point in Florida when there was a loud bang and the whole system went dead. The charger appeared to have tripped a circuit breaker and caused damage to the car storage system. The Bolt was later declared a total insurance loss by the GM dealers. The charger operators, Electrify America are investigating.

431 Pieces of eight

In 1910 American engineer Milton Reeves launched his new car model, designed to cope with the appalling road surfaces of the time. The Reeves Overland Octoauto from Indiana looked like an early brass-era convertible of the time – but with eight wheels. The plan was to even out the rough road surfaces – but just for extra style all eight wheels turned to steer the car.

This made the car very big – almost 21 feet long (6.3m). Sadly the Octoauto failed to attract any buyers.

432 Universal wheels

The only motoring measurement that all the world agrees on isn't speed, distance, engine size or fuel amounts... it's wheel size. All car wheels around the world are described by the diameter in inches.

433 R for records

When five generations of Honda Civic Type-R hot hatches were raced against each other on a drag track testers found the most recent version wasn't the fastest. The 2017 third generation car won the speed test, although all the more recent Type-Rs trounced the earliest models.

434 Tyre take-over

The Michelin brothers took over their father's business making rubber items like belts and pipes in 1886.
Inflatable tyres (Americans, can you put up with the English spelling just for now? I think you can work out that these 'tyres' are the same as your 'tires'.) were a new invention at the time, thanks to John Dunlop's 1888 patent.
But when a cyclist with one of the new type of tyres with a puncture approached them for help, their minds started whirring. Fixing a tyre was a long laborious process at that time.
Andre and Edouard Michelin realised there was great potential in these new inflatable tyres but they needed to be able to be repaired and replaced quickly. If only the wheel or tyre could be detached easily from the vehicle.
They eventually came up with the idea of a detachable tyre and won the patent for it in 1891. That was the start of the Michelin tyre company.

435 Sales pitch

An Australian car-owner recently tried to sell an ageing Ford Falcon by showing a photo of it being pulled over by the police. The Melbourne driver was asking Aus $3,000 (US$2,100/£1,600) for the 1999 152,000km maroon saloon, hoping that a photo of a BMW traffic patrol car with flashing lights and an officer bending to look at the tyres would improve its sales potential. The unusual sales pitch failed to impress buyers though and he instead received teasing messages like: "$3,000? Mate you are dreaming!"

436 Battery-powered Bat

One of the world's first electric vehicles was the strangely-named Electrobat, built in 1894 by American engineer Henry Morris in Philadelphia.

The original was immensely heavy due to its huge lead battery but the design was refined and entered production the following year. The New Jersey car came with early pneumatic tires, rear-wheel steering and a range of 25 miles (42km) between charges. For a while it became popular as a New York cab.

437 Weight loss

Porsche saved weight on the 1967 911R sportscar by ditching the metal 'Porsche' badge and using a sticker instead.

438 Steam power

Some say the very first motorised vehicle was really Cugnot's Locomotive. This was a self-propelled steam gun-carriage devised in 1769 for the French military. It had three wheels, could reach speeds of 2.5mph (4kph) and had to stop every ten minutes to build up enough steam power to get going again.

439 Le Winners

Top ten winners of the Le Mans 24-Hour race:

1.   Porsche (19 times)
2.   Audi (13)
3.   Ferrari (9)
4.   Jaguar (7)
5.   Bentley (6)
6.   Toyota (5)
7.   Alfa Romeo (4) and Ford (4)
8.   Matra Simca (3) and Peugeot (3)

Most consecutive wins is by Porsche (seven)
Most wins by a nationality of team is by Germany (34)
Most wins by a single car type is by Audi R8 (five)
Most participations without winning is by Chevrolet (37)
Driver with most wins is Tom Kristensen (nine)
Nationality with most winning drivers is UK (30)

440 Crystal clear

What would the modern wellness industry have made of hard-nosed Australian racing legend Peter Brock?

In the eighties Brock was a motorsport superstar, known as the "King of the Mountain" for his dominance at Australia's Mount Panorama Circuit, with nine wins at the Bathurst 1000, one at the Bathurst 24 Hour and was a three-time Australian touring car champion.

Brock also helped produce special-edition cars assembled by Holden Dealer Team racing outfit. These primarily took the form of Commodore and Statesmen sedans converted to satisfy motorsports homologation requirements but also to help Holden's prestige on the street.

Roughly 4,000 HDT Special Vehicles were built by the mid-1980s – when Brock was introduced to chiropractor Dr Eric Dowker. The eccentric therapist gradually introduced the racing driver to crystals and their supposed powers to heal. After a couple years of wearing crystal jewellery to 'align his energy', Brock began to apply their powers to his cars. He secretly fitted his HDT race machines with Dowker-supplied crystals.

They were accidentally discovered by a driver after they came loose and flew about the cabin in an accident during testing. Brock came clean. He had been fitting an "Energy Polarizer," a small black box containing crystals and magnets embedded in resin to his race cars. The energy polarizers were attached to the car body in order to improve its performance in some mystical way.

Race-hardened Aussie drivers were soon becoming perplexed by Brock's special polarising rituals like forest ceremonies and the fitting of a small aerial to race cars to 'align their molecules'. Popular driver Larry Perkins left the team shaking his head at this point.

Brock then decided to add the device to the latest HDT Special Vehicle, the Director sedan – offering it to buyers as a $480 option. Brock told Wheels magazine: "It's a magic cure. It makes a shithouse car good." All that needed to happen, apparently, was for the box to touch the car and the vehicle was suddenly better in every way, including speed, fuel consumption, handling and noise.

At this point Holden executives flipped and sought to distance the company from Brock. The decade-long partnership was ended, with Tom Walkinshaw Racing taking over Holden Special Vehicles.

A chastened Brock found himself demoted to modifying Ladas and Fords. Sadly he met an untimely end in a 2006 crash while competing in the Targa West Rally.

Today, however, his Energy Polarizer has legendary status in Australian automotive circles. Examples have become highly sought-after collectibles. Fewer than 150 HDT Directors were ever built with the crystal box and the accessory changes hands among collectors for multiples of its original cost. A brief run of tribute HDT VE-VL Commodores built in 2011 even featured a 'polariser' as an authentic historic feature.

441 High T
In 1920 the global motoring industry was so dominated by one brand that it was estimated that around half all the cars in the world were Model T Fords.

442 Speed quiz
In a questionnaire in 2023, 7% of UK male drivers (corresponding to around 1.2m motorists) admit exceeding 120mph on public roads.

443 All's fair
The tiny Rytecraft Scootacar was built in Britain between 1934 and 1940. It was one of the weirdest cars ever made – because it was built from a fairground dodgem car fitted with wheels and a miniscule 98cc petrol engine. Most were single-seat, open-top, single-gear machines. There was no suspension and the brake automatically applied if you lifted off the accelerator.

444 Rocket science
During the 1950s Ford built Sidewinder missiles.

445 Robot charge

Korean manufacturer Hyundai unveiled a robot that charges your electric car for you at the 2023 Seoul Motor Show. Drivers simply reverse into the bay and the robot opens the charging port. The tricky bit is how its robotic arm uses 3-D cameras and AI to plug the charger exactly into the car's socket. The driver can ignore the whole process until charging is complete.

446 Toy profits

The most sought-after Lego car models are sometimes bought new by investors and resold at a profit.

The most in-demand set is the 1960's Ford Mustang. A survey found that the £119.99 toy fetches up to £179.83 when resold on eBay.

The Lamborghini Sian and Bugatti Chiron models, in contrast, depreciate quickly and are generally sold at a loss.

447 Royal excess

The Bugatti Type 41, known as the Royale, was an enormous luxury car built from 1927 to 1933.

The Royale was 21ft (6.4m) long and weighed more than three tonnes. The huge bonnet housed a 12.7-litre (778cu in) engine.

The prominent radiator motif was a sculpture of an elephant designed by Ettore Bugatti's brother Rembrandt Bugatti, a depressed artist who later killed himself.

Only seven were built, making it one of the rarest and most sought-after vehicles in the world. It is also one of the largest production cars ever sold.

The Great Depression meant that even royalty were deterred from buying the Royale. In the end only three were sold. Bugatti then sold the huge unused engines to be fitted to French trains instead.

448 Name desires

The top five reasons people give for naming their cars:

1 'The name fits the car's personality'
2 'Because of its colour'
3 'I think of my car as a member of the household'
4 'I named it after a character from my favourite film'
5 'I named it after a family member or loved one'

449 Increasing speed

Half of UK drivers (51%) support an increase in the speed limit on the motorway to 80mph, with 29% supporting 90mph and 21% for 100mph.
* 23% of UK males admit to driving over 100mph (161kph) at least once and nearly 10 per cent of males have reached speeds of 120mph (193kph) or more.

450 Ideas man

Considered Australia's most successful inventor but largely unknown in most of the rest of the world, Arthur Bishop's developments in steering are estimated to have been used in about a fifth of the world's cars.
After the Second World War Bishop worked as a globe-trotting consultant to the car industries in the US and UK. By the end of his career he had more than 300 patented inventions in 17 different countries. He always claimed bosses in Detroit resisted many of his suggestions because he was not American.
His biggest invention was the rack-and-pinion steering system which he continually refined throughout his life. His engineering company made many millions every year but Bishop drove a humble Honda claiming "he liked the way it steered."
"What the hell do you do with money, anyway?" he said. "Not much bloody use, except to plough back into inventions."

451 And the winner is...

In 1977 marketing teams promoting the Buick Opel came up with the idea of a national ad campaign based on a five-car showdown against their main competitors from Datsun, VW, Toyota and Subaru. The problem was that in the 'showdown' the Opel came second in Buick's own comparison, behind the VW Rabbit.

Bizarrely General Motors bosses decided to go ahead with the showdown campaign across newspapers and magazines, in the name of honesty. They paid to show their car being awarded a cup for coming second and gifting their German rivals fantastic free publicity.

452 The Lady's Metro

The late Lady Diana Spencer, Princess of Wales, owned several luxury vehicles, including a Jaguar XJS-C, Mercedes Benz SL500 and infamous 'black' Ford Escort RS Turbo.As a less well-known-known teenager however she drove more humble vehicles.

At the age of 18, after attending finishing school in Switzerland, Diana returned to England as a teaching assistant and was often seen driving a blue Renault 5.

In October 1980, BL introduced the Austin Mini Metro. Launched with a huge fanfare, the boxy new hatchback was to intended replace the much-loved Mini. Prince Charles test drove one straight from the British Leyland factory in Longbridge, England. The Prince surprised onlookers by taking the humble hatch on a 20-mile round trip.

Soon after this he bought a £3,495 Metro 1.0L and gave it to the latest object of his affections, the 19-year-old Diana.

As she was now linked to Prince Charles, the red Metro was usually followed by countless cameras. She drove it for around seven months until she sold it in June 1981.

The car had three owners since it left the Royal fleet but has only recorded 30,000 miles. It was sold at auction in the 90s for £6,000. The former Royal hatchback now belongs to the Coventry Transport Museum.

• The Austin Metro was a big seller in Britain, with more than 1 million being sold over a 10-year production run.

• Once a common sight on British roads, the Austin Metro didn't age well. It is now rarely seen and only around 100 are currently registered in the UK.

453 Playboy polymath

Tall, handsome and athletic Spanish playboy aristocrat Alfonso de Portago excelled at everything he tried.

He drove in five F1 Grand Prix races for Ferrari, twice rode horses in the Grand National race at Aintree in England and also led Spain's two-man bobsleigh team to fourth at the 1956 Winter Olympics. The young millionaire was also acclaimed as the best bridge player in the world, was fluent in four languages and won a bet at the age of 17 by flying a plane under London's Tower Bridge.

Alfonso won six major international car races and came second in the British F1 Grand Prix.

The 28-year-old's promising career was tragically ended when a tyre blew while he was driving at 150mph through an Italian village during the 1957 Mille Miglia. The accident killed Alfonso, his navigator and nine spectators, five of them children.

454 Flight of fancy

Before the Second World War Ford built planes as well as cars. Around 200 of the Ford Trimotor aircraft were built between 1925 and 1933, after which Henry Ford started losing interest in the project.

455 Chat GTP takes over

One tired grey morning when I was devoid of inspiration I confess I asked AI language program Chat-GTP for some quirky but true motoring stories.

This is what it came up with:

The Atomic Avenger:
In the midst of Cold War paranoia during the 1950s, a peculiar car model made headlines for its unique feature - a built-in nuclear bomb detector.
Known as the "Atomic Avenger," this extraordinary vehicle was designed by Dr. Henry Monroe, a brilliant scientist with a passion for automotive innovation.
It was in the quiet town of Oakridge, Tennessee, a hub of nuclear research, where Dr. Monroe unveiled his groundbreaking creation. The Atomic Avenger, a sleek and futuristic automobile, boasted a cutting-edge detection system that could sense radiation emitted by nuclear bombs.
Equipped with specialized Geiger counters and state-of-the-art monitoring equipment, the car promised to offer peace of mind during an era of nuclear anxiety.
The Atomic Avenger quickly caught the attention of the public and the media, who marvelled at the audacious invention. It became a symbol of both scientific progress and the prevailing fears of the time. Dr. Monroe's creation garnered widespread interest, prompting other car manufacturers to explore similar technological advancements for civilian use.
Though the Atomic Avenger never saw mass production due to the declining tensions of the Cold War, its legacy endured as a remarkable testament to the ingenuity and innovation of the automotive industry during an extraordinary era in history.

The Revolutionary Roundabout
In a quaint town nestled in the heart of France, an automotive revolution unfolded in the 1920s with the introduction of the first-ever round steering wheel. Le Mans, renowned for its annual 24-hour endurance race, played host to this remarkable development that forever changed the way drivers interacted with their automobiles.

It was on a sunny morning in June 1924 when Monsieur Jacques Renault, a visionary engineer and racing enthusiast, unveiled his groundbreaking invention. The round steering wheel, a departure from the traditional tiller-like controls of early cars, offered drivers improved manoeuvrability, enhanced control, and a more intuitive driving experience. The innovation of the round steering wheel captured the imagination of the motoring world.

As news spread, automakers worldwide scrambled to adopt this ingenious design. It quickly became a defining feature of modern automobiles, shaping the future of driving for generations to come.

Today, as we take for granted the familiar feel of a round steering wheel in our hands, we owe a debt of gratitude to Monsieur Jacques Renault and the revolutionary spirit that transformed the way we navigate the open road.

I hope these stories capture the essence you're looking for, blending humor and historical context with a journalistic touch. Let me know if you'd like more.

…And that, dear reader, was the end of that particular quest. I thought Chat GTP's stories were okay but a bit waffly and cheesily written.

So I gave up on trying to get AI to write the book for me and so now we'll return to the real human input:

456 Escort secret

Tina Kirkpatrick drove around her rural village in England's Hertfordshire for 20 years in an unassuming used Ford Escort. She carefully kept secret from everyone who knew her that her grey W-reg four-door car had an clebrity previous life… belonging to Princess Diana.

In fact Tina's 1.6-litre Ghia car with wood interior trim and blue velour seats had been given to Diana by Prince Charles as an engagement present.

Diana regularly drove the 1980 car to visit Charles and was once photographed arriving in it at a polo match. Her sister Sarah Spencer gave her a small silver frog mascot that Diana attached to the front of the bonnet.

Di eventually sold it two months after giving birth to Prince William in 1982.

It ended up with an antique dealer in 1995 before being sold to Mrs Kirkpatrick, who is a keen fan of Princess Diana.

She told reporters: "A lot of people ask me why I had it and I used to tell them that it was my first car I passed my test in and that I was attached to it. I felt that its history and provenance were so unique and I didn't want many people knowing."

Mrs Kirkpatrick finally decided to sell the car to an unknown buyer for £40,000 in 2021.

457 W-power

The Mercedes W125 racing car of 1937 produced an extraordinary amount of power for the era: 637bhp.

This power level was the highest in Grand Prix racing for half a century, until it was finally surpassed by the turbocharged Formula One cars of the 1980s.

Unsurprisingly, the silver torpedo-shaped car dominated the racing world at the time. It won the 1937 European Championship. And it also came second, third and fourth.

458 Natural badges

In 2022 the Romanian budget marque Dacia re-branded itself. It changed its traditional shield logo for the word 'Dacia' written in a futuristic script.

On the cars themselves the Dacia badge colours changed from silver and blue to khaki green, which the company's PR department claimed "evokes the brand's closeness to nature."

459 Getting tyred

The first patent for radial tyres was issued in 1914 but they weren't introduced on American cars for more than half a century after that.

For decades US tyre makers were able to get away with maintaining a monopoly, selling cheaply-made tyres of thin rubber that generally lasted less than year.

Finally the unlikely saviour arrived: Sears retail chain began offering imported Michelin radial tyres in 1966. These advanced steel-belted radial tyres had been available for more than a decade in Europe.

The results were dramatic: American tyre life immediately doubled, fuel consumption fell and driving was much safer. Within nine years 90% of new American cars were fitted with radial tyres.

460 Stout proposition

The Stout Scarab was launched in 1932 and instantly became one of the weirdest-looking cars of all time.

The unibody aluminium aircraft-style cylindrical body designed by William Stout had a Ford V8 at the back, bluff front end and tapered rear. It offered seats for six, reversible chairs, a table – and a huge price tag equivalent to over $100,000 today.

If that wasn't tricky enough commercially, it was primarily marketed as an office on wheels. Only nine were built but five are believed to still exist in American museums and collections.

461 Light delay

The 1966 British luxury coupe the Jensen Interceptor was the first car with a 'courtesy interior light' that stayed on for a while after you got out of the car.

462 Polar record

The speed record of crossing Antarctica from the McMurdo Station on the coast to the South Pole (an arduous journey of about 1,000 miles) was broken recently – by a Ford E-Series van.

The modified E-Series, with six-wheel-drive, 20-speed gearbox and a 7.3-litre V8, achieved the crossing in 70 hours. The previous driving record was 24 days.

463 Bear necessities

When Nevada police found a large bear trapped inside a family SUV outside a home in Washoe County they cleared the area, tied a rope to the door handle and retreated a safe distance.

Video footage showed that when they pulled the rope, the boor burst open and the bear leapt out. It immediately ran into nearby woods, leaving a torn and mutilated car interior behind.

464 Less Lancias

The elegant and sporty Lancia Prisma saloon was the brand's top-selling model in the UK in the 1980s.

Rust problems and unreliability shortened the Italian car's lifespan so drastically that a recent report found that there are only four Prismas left on British roads.

465 Toy shots

A middle-aged university worker from Edinburgh, Scotland, started taking photos of his son's Hot Wheels miniature toy cars for fun while out on walks during the Covid pandemic. The casual experiment grew into an obsession and Ross Burns has ended up taking 1,000 different photos of toy cars in different locations around Britain.

The three-year project included sprawling on the pavement to take increasingly close-up life-like shots of toy cars outside Buckingham Palace in London and on the dockside in Leith, Scotland. "When I go away for a couple of days, the first thing I pack are the Hot Wheels," he said.

466 Legal term

The phrase 'joy-riding' was coined by a judge in New York dealing with taking and driving away offences... in 1908.

467 Motor city

More than half the 44,000 population of Mlada Boleslav in the Czech Republic works for Skoda.

468 Zoe continues

Renault is not an uncommon French surname. When the French car-maker Renault announced a new car would be called the Renault Zoe, two sets of parents with the surname Renault objected. They had already called their daughters Zoe.

The Renaults took Renault to court. The families claimed the new car name would expose their children to ridicule. Their solicitor told the court the children, and any others called Zoe, would face a lifetime of ridicule. Playground teasing and bar banter might include: "Can I see your airbags?" or "Can I shine your bumper?" he claimed.

The judge dismissed their claims and allowed Renault to continue to launch the new Zoe.

469 Plane sailing

French engineer Marcel Leyat set out to build a pioneering aircraft in 1909 but ran out of money. So he created a car that looked like a plane without wings.

His Helica was made of wood and was powered by a large propellor at the front. The light weight meant a Helica could reach 106mph/170kph – and 30 were built. Today four Helicas still survive.

470 The worst drivers of all time

A YouTube channel called The Fancy Banana compiled clips of 'the worst 20 drivers of all time'.

It's actually a bit long and boring, plus the voice-over is unbearably cheesy but the stories are pretty good. I've summarised them.

Here they are:

20 A young blonde Spanish woman ignores a warning sign and drives into a flooded underpass that is so deep her car starts floating away.

She is forced to climb out the window and haul herself on to the roof of the red hatchback. It floats under the flooded flyover with her standing and trying to balance awkwardly on the roof, which is almost underwater by now.

Finally firefighters arrive, wade into the shoulder-deep water to her car. She climbs onto a firefighter's shoulders and is walked to safety.

19 A 56-year-old Dutch man drives towards automatic swing bridge and rather wait for it to close tries to accelerate and leap across the five-meter gap.

His stationwagon doesn't make it, smashes into the side of the roadway opposite and plunges into the water below. The car sinks but he is rescued by lifeguards.

18 CCTV cameras catch a male BMW driver in Slovakia who suffered momentary microsleep at 5am one morning, accidentally mounted a kerbside ramp and took off, and woke to finding he was 20 feet into the air, flying through the mouth of a road tunnel, turning over and then sliding along the tunnel roadway on its roof. Amazingly the 44-year-old local driver escaped with minor scratches.

17 More overhead CCTV camera footage shows an unnamed male driver humiliatingly trying to park his large white SUV in a large space between two other vehicles.
He tries 15 times and even enlists passers-by to direct him before giving up, parking side on at the entrance to the car park and walking off looking frustrated.
The footage was leaked to YouTube where it soon gathered around 90 million views.

16 A 94-year-old man in a white Oldsmobile confuses his pedals and presses the accelerator by mistake and races through the Quick Quack car wash in Sacremento, California at over 40mph, breaking off the rotary brushes, smashing side water hoses and causing about $100,000-worth of damage.
He then smashes straight into the car park wall beyond.
The driver was unhurt. The car-wash owner ingeniously used the security camera footage to make a highly successful commercial for his business.

15 Footage shot by a resident out on their balcony above a busy narrow street in Naples shows yet another white car, this time a Fiat 500 – and what is described as 'Italy's worst driver'. This is my favourite of all these clips.

The Fiat driver apparently tries a U-turn in the middle of the very narrow street but gets jammed at 90 degrees to the road between parked cars on either side.

Crowds of pedestrians join in, shouting, waving arms and giving useless directions. The car tries over-and-over to inch out of the awkward jam.

Waiting cars in both directions blare horns at the hold up. The final indignity is that a pedestrian church funeral procession appears round the corner, with priests, mourners and a decorated coffin walking along the street with a police escort. They march slowly toward the helpless trapped car. The policemen and clergymen eventually manage to help the driver manoeuvre free.

14 A grey Peugeot tries to parallel park in a large disabled space in a busy tree-lined street – trying over and over for seven minutes. The embarrassing footage shows the car at 45 degrees, trying to approach from both directions, reversing in, driving in forwards but always apparently ending up at 45 degrees to the pavement.

The climax is when the car in the space in front moves away creating an enormous gap four or five times as long as the car – but the Peugeot driver still can't manage to position his car correctly.

13 A man test-driving a red Ferrari California open-top supercar around the streets of the company's hometown of Maranello in Italy is filmed by a camera at the back of the car. He almost loses control several times in innocuous traffic situations before taking a simple suburban corner too fast, spinning and hitting a garden wall. We don't know the names or details, we only see the expensive embarrassment.

12 A home doorbell camera captures an extraordinary night-time scene at a sleepy ranch-style house in Santa Fe Springs, California. Out of nowhere a speeding car appears, hits the garden wall and takes off, flying over the garden and embedding itself into the side of the house.
The male driver is then seen climbing from the rubble and running from the scene.

11 Oklahoma police video footage shows the aftermath of a truck driver losing control and overturning. His cargo – a swarm of honey bees – escaped and completely cover the front of the police response vehicle.

10 A Fed Ex delivery driver pulls up to a house in Tennessee USA, gets out in readiness to make a delivery but hasn't put the vehicle in park or applied the handbrake. The house security camera shows him desperately try to hold on to the door to stop the van's movement as it starts rolling backwards but it accelerates.
The delivery man appears to drop his phone and gives up holding on to the accelerating van. It rolls back across another road, trundles across a garden, narrowly missing another house, rolls between trees and crosses another road, backwards, and comes to rest in the distance against a fence.

9 The driver of a green Pontiac turns in a car park and slowly drives into the three-bay mechanic's workshop. A mechanic guides him slowly in but suddenly the car seems accelerate madly, the front wheel goes straight into the inspection pit and the whole car topples over sideways into the hole.

8 An internal surveillance camera shows staff serving customers at the counter Mighty-O Donuts in downtown Seattle. Suddenly a silver SUV bursts through the shop wall. Customers try to cover their heads and staff hide down beneath the counter as dust and glass shower in all directions. The vehicle comes to rest next to the counter and somehow escapes with minor injuries.

7 A recently-qualified female driver in a large black executive saloon is shown smashing into three stationary cars while trying to park, knocking two of them violently sideways, and then reverses rapidly, demolishing a ten-foot high wall of a building whose roof rather comically collapses on top of the car.

6 Dashcam footage of a rainy day in Washington DC shows a grey saloon driving straight into the front store window of a Subway outlet on a busy city street.
The crashed car immediately reverses out of the Subway store, across two lanes of traffic and impales its trunk on a lamppost of the McDonald's car park on the other side of the road. The dashcam car holds back, understandably nervous about what is going to happen next.

5 A female driver catches her heel between two pedals, driving her large silver luxury company saloon onto the pavement, knocking down a traffic sign (warning of pedestrians crossing) and continues right through a shop window. No-one was seriously injured in this spectacular event in Bosnia.

4 A traffic camera shows a Chinese bus driver realise he was soon approaching a multi-lane highway tollbooth that his vehicle couldn't fit through. So he decides to make a u-turn on the busy four-lane road. The large purple coach blocks all the lanes as it turns – then tries to work its way back through four lanes of on-coming traffic.

3 A woman driver is shown heading to work in California in a brand new white Toyota CHR SUV that she's just brought. She isn't used to the automatic controls and while trying to forward park reverses instead.
She careers across the car park, panics and presses the accelerator. This causes her to smash through the multi-storey car-park wall at speed and end up 50ft off the ground with two wheels dangling off the side of the fourth-level of the building. Her door handle was ripped off as she scraped against a concrete pillar so she was trapped inside and had to be rescued, unhurt but shocked, from the passenger side. Her dramatic mistakes were captured for all to see on the car park security video.

2 A young woman was shopping for a new Honda in a smart dealership in Northern India. A salesman encourages the woman to sit in a new silver i20 hatchback.
She seems to accidentally press the accelerator as she gets into the driver's seat – and, as the salesman holds his head in horror, the car accelerates across the showroom, smashes through a plate glass wall, down some steps and out into the car park where it crashes into two other cars. Eventually she comes to rest between the two mangled cars where she emerges apparently unhurt but looking shocked.

1 An elderly lady driver in the Denver, Colorado suburbs mysteriously drove across grass, between tress and through bushes… right into a house's swimming pool. Her silver saloon was poignantly shown submerged in the pool in news drone footage.

471 Lost in time

A third of British drivers nostalgically look back to a time when they could tinker with the car's engine on the drive (33%), wind-down windows by hand (30%) and only have to use four gears (21%). A quarter (25%) even miss having to manually lock the car with a key.

A poll of motorists found that drivers also miss their old car stereos, with nearly a fifth (19%) missing their car cassette player and more than a tenth (13%) missing manually tuning the radio.

* Two-thirds (69%) of drivers think modern technology makes drivers lazy and when it comes to cars today, three fifths (62%) could happily live without lane assist technology, over half (52%) would not miss distance assist, and two fifths (44%) would be happy without automatic braking.

472 Coat of many colours

Bosses at Dodge made a special promotional model of the Challenger muscle car in 2023 – painted with 25 stripes. Each stripe was one of the official optional factory colours, including hues like gold metallic, rallye red, alpine white, lime green metallic and black velvet.

The weird-looking harlequin paintjob turned out to be a surprise hit with Challenger fans. It was so popular that Dodge now offers the multicoloured striped finish as an option in its own right.

473 Dogs body

One of the earliest British motor cars, the 1902 Glasgow-built Arrol-Johnston, was nicknamed the 'dogcart'.

It featured a distinctive wooden body with a surprising unusual feature: the driver with the steering wheel, brake levers and controls were positioned in the back row of seats. A row of passenger seats were positioned in front of the driver.

474 Drunk and disqualified

Colourful Jaguar works drivers Tony Rolt and Duncan Hamilton thought they had been disqualified on the eve of the Le Mans 24 Hour Race in 1953.

Rolt, a former Colditz prisoner of war who escaped from seven different German camps, and Hamilton, a heroic former wartime pilot, unwittingly had been practicing in a Jaguar C-Type which had the same racing number as another car. This is forbidden in the rules. The duo went to a bar to drown their disappointment, unaware they had since been re-instated by officials.

A few hours before the race Jaguar team bosses tracked the depressed duo down in a local bar, allegedly drunk. They gave them the news: "Get back to the pits, you're supposed to be taking part in the Le Mans 24-hour race."

The pair rushed back to the track and started the race. The Jaguar crew tried to use the pit stops to give Hamilton coffee to sober him up – but he refused saying 'it made his arms twitch'. Instead, bizarrely, they gave him brandy.

Amazingly it worked. When Hamilton hit a bird at full speed down the Mulsanne Straight in his open-top car it broke his nose. But he didn't lose control and drove on straight regardless. Somehow the duo sped four laps ahead of an identical Jaguar driven by Stirling Moss. Rolt and Hamilton went on to win the prestigious 24-hour race – and set a new record time. They were first to record an average time of over 100mph for the 24 hours.

• Duncan Hamilton's race career was full of similar colourful mishaps. His nickname was 'Drunken Hamilton'. Later in 1953 he lost control during the Portuguese Grand Prix, crashed off the track into an electricity pylon and cut off power to the city of Porto for hours. He was thrown from the car and ended up hanging from a tree. He eventually wiggled free but fell onto the track and had to quickly move his legs to avoid being run over by a Ferrari.

475 We are all doomed

Boffins from the Cambridge Research Group IDTechEx produced a report on the future of road transport in Summer 2023. The academics predicted that by 2050 all human driving will be outlawed.

The scientists judged that autonomous cars will match or exceed human safety by 2024. The group claimed in their report 'Autonomous Cars, Robotaxis & Sensors 2022–2042' that by the 2040s, autonomous cars will be capable of fulfilling the world's mobility needs without a single collision. "So why should humans be allowed to continue driving?" it concludes.

The End

Printed in Great Britain
by Amazon

35133626R00116